TAMING

THE

SABERTOOTH

TAMING
— THE —
SABERTOOTH

RESILIENT LEADERSHIP
IN A STRESSFUL WORLD

TRACEY GROVE

Advantage®

Published by Advantage, Charleston, South Carolina.
Member of Advantage Media Group.

ADVANTAGE is a registered trademark, and the Advantage colophon is a trademark of Advantage Media Group, Inc.

Printed in the United States of America.

10 9 8 7 6 5 4 3 2 1

ISBN: 978-1-64225-070-1
LCCN: 2019933662

Book design by Carly Blake.

This publication is designed to provide accurate and authoritative information in regard to the subject matter covered. It is sold with the understanding that the publisher is not engaged in rendering legal, accounting, or other professional services. If legal advice or other expert assistance is required, the services of a competent professional person should be sought.

Advantage Media Group is proud to be a part of the Tree Neutral® program. Tree Neutral offsets the number of trees consumed in the production and printing of this book by taking proactive steps such as planting trees in direct proportion to the number of trees used to print books. To learn more about Tree Neutral, please visit www.treeneutral.com.

Advantage Media Group is a publisher of business, self-improvement, and professional development books and online learning. We help entrepreneurs, business leaders, and professionals share their Stories, Passion, and Knowledge to help others Learn & Grow. Do you have a manuscript or book idea that you would like us to consider for publishing? Please visit advantagefamily.com or call 1.866.775.1696.

To Peter: my husband, my partner in life, and
my best friend. This wouldn't have been possible without
your wisdom, intellectual insight, and unflagging support.
This book is for you, with love always.

TABLE OF CONTENTS

FOREWORD

When I wrote *The Stirring of the Soul in the Workplace* almost twenty-five years ago, the importance of meaning, joy, and purpose at work was a conversation that was just beginning. I was inviting a dialogue about thriving as a whole person but was often asked "How can we just leave people's personality at the door?" The workplace is still a challenging environment confronting continual change, volatility, and uncertainty. What is different today is that we have much greater clarity about the behaviors and mind-set that make a difference. Our approach to work, the ways we construct meaning, the emotional resilience we cultivate, and how we collaborate with others, is fundamental to both well-being and accomplishment. They affect how we feel every day and how successfully we perform in our roles. They affect how we interact with others and how groups within an organization act together for achieving goals. Most critically, they influence how we maintain our sanity, move beyond failures, and achieve some measure of gratitude for the successes we have and the people we work with.

Tracey Grove's *Taming the Sabertooth: Resilient Leadership in a Stressful World* is a shining example of how far we have come. She is a natural storyteller gifted with the ability to make meaning and show us alternative ways of coping, communicating, and caring while committing to a better workplace environment. She shares critical knowledge about the neuroscience of threat, the psychology of performance, and the growing research on resilience in simple and digestible ways that easily lead to personal action. I highly recommend this as a primer for workplace survival and a guide to cultivating your best self. If this book was around twenty-five years ago, fewer people would have worried about leaving the whole person outside the workplace doors.

Alan Briskin, PhD
Author, *The Stirring of Soul in the Workplace*
Co-Author, *Daily Miracles, Bringing Your Soul to Work*, and *The Power of Collective Wisdom*

THE TERRIFYING TALE
OF THE SABERTOOTH

Throughout human history, we have had to deal with physical threats in our environment. When we were running around in the wild and a hungry saber-toothed cat saw us as a delicious snack, we had a split second to decide whether to fight an opponent we stood no chance of defending against, run in the opposite direction, or hide behind a rock attempting to be invisible. This is the fight-flight-freeze response hardwired into our brains that is activated in response to any perceived threat.

Today, the sabertooth looks very different. It takes the form of business competition, shifting marketplaces, and rapid digital transformation. It looks much like an overflowing email inbox, a challenging performance assessment, a difficult client meeting, a conflict with a colleague, or an organizational shift. All these daily stressors trigger the same response in our primitive brain, as our amygdala, the tiny almond-shaped mass of nuclei located deep within the temporal lobes of our brain responsible for emotional and social processing, is hijacked. Neurons in the amygdala are responsible for fear-conditioning and will activate our fight-flight-freeze response when we sense a threat. Through this activation, our "feeling brain" is cut off from our "thinking brain," as the prefrontal cortex, responsible for complex processes such as memory, planning, reasoning, and problem-solving shuts down, and our amygdala takes over.

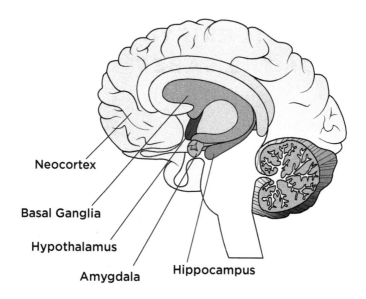

Neocortex

Basal Ganglia

Hypothalamus

Amygdala   Hippocampus

"Amygdala hijack" is a term coined by Daniel Goleman in his 1996 book *Emotional Intelligence: Why It Can Matter More Than IQ*. Drawing on the work of Joseph E. LeDoux, Goleman used the term to describe emotional responses that are immediate and overwhelming. The response is often out of proportion to the actual stimulus because it has triggered a much more significant emotional threat.

This survival mechanism lets us react to events before the rational brain has time to mull things over. And this automatic fight-flight-freeze response is still mobilized when we perceive any threat. The difference is that in contrast to the *physical* threats our ancestors encountered that would result in some form of physiological response (fight-flight-freeze), our largely *psychological* stressors today rarely give us the same opportunity (we can't have brawls in the boardroom). Our ancestors could shed the cortisol and adrenaline that stress had built up through running or some other form of extreme labor, but today we have no quick way to expend the excess energy and stress hormones generated by our typical response to stress.

It's this constant cycle of sustained mobilization without any release that prolongs psychological stress and causes strain on our cardiovascular and immune systems, spilling into every area of our lives. The sabertooth has evolved. Unfortunately, our response to it hasn't. Until now.[1]

---

1   "Understanding the stress response," Harvard Health Publishing, last modified May 1, 2018, https://www.health.harvard.edu/staying-healthy/understanding-the-stress-response.

INTRODUCTION

HIDING BEHIND A ROCK
IS NOT AN OPTION

A defining moment in my life came on May 21, 1998 when my husband, Peter, and I were victims of a carjacking in South Africa. On a quiet Thursday night like any other, a single event radically changed our lives and set us on an entirely new path. Ultimately, becoming survivors of a traumatic event that should have taken our lives gave us both a new perspective and appreciation for life. It also made me curious about resilience. It was a topic I felt called to understand more deeply and to write about in a time when stress and anxiety are increasingly becoming issues in the world: Can we learn to deal with stress in a healthy way?

Increased competition, longer working hours, and higher performance expectations are all contributing to a stressful work environment. And the news at home isn't much better. Digitization and always-on technology have blurred the boundaries between our work and personal lives, removing the natural buffer between them and costing us our health. We all know fear, disappointment, and heartache. And we all experience joy, optimism, and happiness. What I wanted to find out was how we can learn to build a more optimistic outlook as a buffer when times get tough. We can't necessarily change our environment, but we have the power to shift our response to that environment by building resilience.

This need for understanding resilience set me on the path to learn more than I could ever have imagined—going back to school to earn a second bachelor's degree in psychology, a master's in organizational development and leadership, and a professional coaching certification—all with the singular focus of learning about a human being's capability to deal with adversity.

Two decades of experience working in both public and private sectors has given me the benefit of dealing with individual and interpersonal issues, communication challenges, and organizational shifts first-hand. Over the years, I developed my Taming the Sabertooth resilience workshop, applying many of the lessons learned through relationships with colleagues and clients that both challenged and inspired me. Working with leaders from the C-suite down through every level of organizations, leveraging positive psychology, neuroscience, and cognitive-behavioral techniques helps individuals, teams and leaders build their resilience muscle and accelerate performance.

I have had the opportunity to learn from leaders from all over the world. And have had the privilege of coaching many of them as they worked to build resilient organizations through clarity, authenticity, and humility. It is incredibly rewarding to help individuals find their voice and take their performance to levels of which they didn't believe they were capable.

THIS BOOK IS FOR YOU

So that's what this book is about: all the lessons learned about resilience, courage, and leadership over the years, working with incredible people across industries, geographies, and cultures. This book is for anyone looking to develop the ability to deal with ambiguity, change, and adversity with courage and grace. If you are a leader struggling to overcome fear and grow your business, a small business owner looking to create a culture you can be proud of, or an individual looking to take your performance to a new level, this book is for you. Individuals, teams, or leaders who wish to better serve others through enhanced communication and a more optimistic outlook will all benefit from this book.

> IF YOU ARE A LEADER STRUGGLING TO OVERCOME FEAR AND GROW YOUR BUSINESS, A SMALL BUSINESS OWNER LOOKING TO CREATE A CULTURE YOU CAN BE PROUD OF, OR AN INDIVIDUAL LOOKING TO TAKE YOUR PERFORMANCE TO A NEW LEVEL, THIS BOOK IS FOR YOU.

You'll learn a set of guiding principles around becoming more resilient in both leadership and everyday life. Building resilience requires focused attention, persistence, and practice. To bounce back from bumps in the road, we all must be prepared to overcome the unexpected. Resilience isn't a single skill; it's a variety of skills and coping mechanisms. So, to break it down, we'll align our exploration of resilience to four fundamentals. These are the Four Cs of Resilience. They are also the four parts of the book:

1. **Communicate**—Communicate with clarity, humility, and authenticity to inspire others to follow.

2. **Challenge**—Be courageous in turbulent times, challenging assumptions and choosing optimism to move through change.

3. **Control**—Move through fear and harness motivation to find the silver lining.

4. **Commit**—Commit to the journey by renewing resources to nurture recovery.

We'll also address Five Truths within in the coming pages:

1. **Change is the new constant**—the world isn't going to slow down anytime soon. We're all going to fall occasionally. Getting up is up to us.

2. **Stress is a necessary part of our lives**—harnessing the sweet spot that boosts performance means stepping over the line.

3. **Resilience takes reinforcement**—neurons that fire together, wire together. It takes practice, persistence, and grit to build your resilience muscle.

4. **Take care of yourself first**—learning to respond and not react puts your oxygen mask on first so you can help others survive the solar flare.

5. **The sabertooth is a kitten**—shifting your perspective and focusing on strengths breaks the stress cycle and lets you tame the sabertooth.

The physical, emotional, and intellectual aspects of building resilience are applicable to every industry and walk of life. Every time I work with clients, I learn much more than I could ever imagine, and the gifts of many of those lessons are in the book. I have experimented with and benefited from the skills and approaches I share in my own life, and I have seen clients take control and shift their perspectives with powerful positive results. I hope that you will have a similar experience.

THREE WAYS TO GET THE MOST OUT OF THIS BOOK

Be open. You may not agree with everything in this book, but please be open to at least considering an alternate approach to work and life. No doubt everyone will get something different from the book.

Shift your perspective. Try out the ideas and concepts that we'll cover and see what fits your unique situation best, and then choose what works for you. Not everything will work for everyone, and that's OK.

Practice persistence. Resilience takes practice—it's not about perfection. When you inevitably encounter your own sabertooth, and your first instinct is to run, freeze or fight, be gentle with yourself. Aristotle says, "We are what we repeatedly do. Excellence then, is not an act, but a habit." Pick yourself up, dust yourself off, and keep going.

Do or Do Not. There is No Try.
—Yoda

PART I

COMMUNICATE WITH CLARITY, HUMILITY, AND AUTHENTICITY TO INSPIRE OTHERS TO FOLLOW

HOW RESILIENT ARE YOU?

Measuring your resilience is the first step to understanding where you have strengths to be optimized and opportunities to shore up your resources.

Rate each item for how true it is for you, using the following scale:

1 = not true of me at all

2 = moderately true of me

3 = very true of me

8/3/21

1. ___2___ I can control the way I feel when I am faced with adversity.

2. ___2___ Even if I plan ahead for a conversation with my boss, a coworker, my spouse, or my child, I still find myself reacting emotionally.

3. ___2___ If someone does something that upsets me, I am able to wait until I have calmed down to discuss it at an appropriate time.

4. ___3___ I often get overwhelmed with negative thoughts when things go wrong.

5. ___1___ When I discuss a difficult topic with a colleague or family member, I can keep my emotions in check.

6. ___2___ My emotions affect my ability to focus on what I need to get done at work, home, or school.

7. ___3___ I believe that problems are controllable, even if I am not always able to change a situation.

8. ___3___ When someone overreacts to an issue, I assume that they are just having a bad day and it's not personal.

9. ___2___ I believe that most problems are caused by circumstances outside my control.

10. ___1___ I have no idea why most people react to issues the way they do.

Add your scores for items 1, 3, 5, 7, and 8 ___11___

Add your scores for items 2, 4, 6, 9 and 10 ___10___

Subtract the bottom score from the top score ___1___

SCORE YOURSELF

4 or below: You tend to perceive stress as all encompassing, which may leave you feeling isolated, overburdened, and helpless. See if the strategies in this book can help you shift your mind-set.

Between 5 and 7: You are mostly optimistic, but the feeling can be undercut by situations that you feel you cannot control. Try out a few of the suggestions in this book to help shore up your resilience.

8 and up: You're already reasonably resilient. You frame stress positively to bounce back from hardship. You may tend to forget to take care of yourself, however, which increases your risk of burnout. Find out how to nurture your recovery.

CHAPTER 1

LIFE (AND WORK) TAKES COURAGE

Resilience is, of course, necessary for a warrior.
But a lack of empathy isn't.
—Phil Klay

The light glinted off the barrel of the gun pointed at me as I reluctantly handed over my wedding ring. Thursday, May 21, 1998 had started out like any other Thursday. My husband, Peter, and I were returning home from our favorite seafood place with our weekly fish-and-chip takeout. We had no idea that the events which were about to unfold would change our lives forever.

Pulling into our driveway at home, we were confronted by five armed, balaclava-wearing men in an all-too-familiar scene of carjacking in South Africa. To provide some additional context for this scene, it's worth mentioning that in South Africa, many carjacking syndicates are well funded (often with the blessing of a corrupt government) and well trained. The gang accosting us appeared to be no exception, executing the robbery with military precision (and brandishing firearms of the type used by the South African police).

We were unarmed, outnumbered, and caught completely off guard. In less than ten minutes, Peter and I had been stripped of wedding rings, wallets, and car keys.

A DIVERGENT PATH

Knowing with absolute certainty that you're about to die is a strange feeling. Victims of carjackings in South Africa are often summarily executed, making for a clean getaway with no one to report the crime until after the carjackers are long gone. The reality of this being our last moment together struck me like ice as Peter and I were told to kneel on the ground. I took comfort from the thought that if this was to be our final moment, at least we would die together. As we waited for the fatal gunshot, I locked eyes for several seconds with our would-be executioner. In that moment of absolute silence, he hesitated, lowered his gun, and made his getaway with the rest of the gang. Astonishingly, the final bullet never came.

We learned from the police that the gang who had accosted us always executed their victims. The police asked what we had done differently to make the gang change what had, until now, been a successful modus operandi. Very few victims had survived the experience. We had both been calm and cooperative, but there was no common denominator to explain why we were still alive.

When the police informed us later that the security guard at the entrance to our gated community had been bribed or coerced to let the gang in, another possibility occurred to me. In the five years we had lived there, Peter and I had always been friendly to the security guard, taking the time to get to know him and asking about his family. We gave him cool drinks on long, hot days, and during the bitterly cold winters when he was shivering in his unheated guard hut, we had brought him hot soup. Was it these simple acts of kindness that had made the difference? Had the security guard negotiated for our lives? We may never know for sure, but I like to think so.

NEW BEGINNINGS

I realized through this experience that you can make a choice to set aside your fear and take the good from what happens to you. Despite a sleepless night after our attack, both Peter and I were back at work early the next morning as usual. We continued on with our lives as we had, albeit with a

> YOU CAN MAKE A CHOICE TO SET ASIDE YOUR FEAR AND TAKE THE GOOD FROM WHAT HAPPENS TO YOU.

heightened awareness of our surroundings. We also learned that the corrupt judicial system in South Africa at that time leaned in favor of the perpetrators, concerned with their government-funded defense and well-being, rather than that of the victims. We eventually made the decision to uproot and start our lives over in the United Kingdom. Moving from South Africa to the United Kingdom was an enormous culture shock. We literally arrived in the UK with nothing but our suitcases, determined to start over again. I was fortunate enough to secure employment with Microsoft in the UK, and seven years later, we were transferred to Washington State in the United States.

Happily settled close to Seattle since then, I became increasingly interested in the neuroscience of adversity and its connection to resilience. I noticed how few of the people around me seemed happy, despite living in what I believe is the greatest country in the world. They had so much to be grateful for, and yet they seemed unsatisfied. They were all chasing the next big thing and being worn down in the process. Could they learn to recognize and appreciate the good in their lives? Could this help them face adversity with courage? As many as 90 percent of trauma survivors report at least some benefit from struggling to deal with the experience, according to research by the University of North Carolina, Charlotte.[2] I wanted to find out if people could learn the skill of resilience without having to go through a traumatic experience.

RESILIENCE THROUGH EMPATHY

Empathy is a powerful emotion. It is one of the strongest ways we can connect to another human being. It connects us with others by making us more willing to see another point of view. Seeing life through the eyes of others helps us to appreciate what we have, and to become kinder and more giving. I believe that showing empathy to a security guard in South Africa saved our lives. As I researched empathy, a consistent theme emerged; it cannot co-exist with fear. Empathy builds courage, and courage builds resilience. Showing kindness to others is an act of love, and in doing so, we overcome fear, become kinder to ourselves, and we become happier.

My curiosity about behavior in stressful situations turned into years of learning about a human being's ability to withstand adversity. I wanted to help individuals and organizations not only survive a stressful environment but thrive in spite of it. In 2008, I founded Pure Symmetry Coaching and focused my research on the connection between resilience and high performance. I discovered one thing that was unexpected and surprising (and that my clients are always disappointed to learn). Stress is absolutely necessary.

---

2   Richard G. Tedeschi, "Violence Transformed: Posttraumatic Growth in Survivors and Their Societies," *Aggression and Violent Behavior* 4, no. 3 (1999): 319-41, https://ptgi.uncc.edu/wp-content/uploads/sites/9/2015/01/ Violence-transformed-Posttraumatic-growth-in-survivors-and-their-societies.pdf.

THE STRESS PARADOX

Our brains are wired in such a way that it's impossible to take any action until we feel at least some level of stress.[3] Studies have found that the onset of stress entices the brain into growing new cells that are responsible for improved memory. Performance peaks under the heightened activation that comes with moderate levels of stress, as you can see from the stress curve diagram below. If the stress isn't prolonged, it's harmless. And that's where we run into a problem.

STRESS CURVE

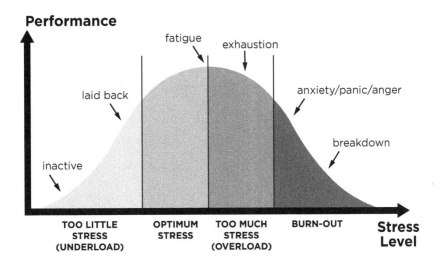

The paradox of stress is that it's beneficial effect only works when the stress is intermittent. As soon as it continues beyond a few moments into a prolonged state, stress counteracts the brain's ability to develop those new memory cells and suppresses performance.[4] We need stress to perform well, but only so much of it helps us do so.

---

3   Robert Sanders, "Researchers find out why some stress is good for you," Berkeley News, April 16, 2013, https://news.berkeley.edu/2013/04/16/researchers-find-out-why-some-stress-is-good-for-you/.

4   "How repeated stress impairs memory," Science Daily, March 7, 2012, https://www.sciencedaily.com/releases/2012/03/120307132202.html.

If we have too little stress, we can experience boredom and apathy. We can become disinterested and disengaged from things we enjoy or that we know are good for us. The less we exercise, the more weary and worn out (and overweight) we become, and the less we feel inclined to exercise. The less we are pushed into action because of too little stress, the more inactivated we become.

Optimal stress is where our performance is at its best, where we feel capable, and where we are activated in a healthy way for a short period of time. But we can quickly move into too much stress and become overloaded. We start to feel fatigued, and if the stress continues, we risk becoming mentally and physically exhausted.

It becomes a slippery slope as the stressful situation persists, and—as it tries to adapt—our body enters a stage of resistance. Our immune system becomes impaired, and we become vulnerable to diseases of adaptation such as ulcers, high blood pressure, and asthma, along with issues like adrenal failure. We become sick—physically, mentally, and emotionally. We're on the road to breakdown. The antithesis of this situation is resilience.

Resilience helps us withstand crisis, adapt to change, and rebound from challenges and adversity. It shifts our response to situations that feel threatening to our primitive brains and helps us to stay in optimal performance, avoiding both boredom and burnout. By challenging our assumptions, choosing our responses, and committing to our recovery, we can increase our performance, balance, and happiness at work and at home. This creates a courageous mind-set and transforms the way we engage with the world around us.

THREE CALLS TO ACTION

1. Be open to new ideas and new ways of learning. Embrace a new perspective and have fun with it. You may discover something surprising.

2. Lean into the stress curve. Understand where you are on the curve and what is keeping you there. Then you can work to change it.

3. Be kind to yourself by being kind to others. Empathy builds courage, and courage builds resilience.

CHAPTER 2

AN INVITATION TO COMMUNICATE DIFFERENTLY

Clients do not come first. Employees come first. If you take care of your employees, they will take care of the clients.
—Richard Branson

Regardless of what business we are in, the ability to react quickly and adapt is critical. As technology and disruptive forces increase the pace of change, we have to find new ways to communicate and work together. This takes a new approach to leadership, one that emphasizes personal connection with our employees, our customers, and our partners.

THE LOST ART

Personal connection becomes more elusive as we become more technology-driven as a society. In meetings, we're keeping an eye on our screens, more focused on email than the conversation in the room. Go to a social gathering, and chances are you'll see people huddled over their handheld devices or phones. We're physically together, but we're really alone. Have we lost the ability to connect human to human?

I started my career long before the days of email, the internet, or even Microsoft Windows. I remember when connecting to the internet via dial-up was state of the art, and you would have to wait patiently for the high-pitched modem screech to signal a connection. It was such simple technology, but even then, we were held hostage by it. When I started working in a high-tech company that had instant messenger, this dependence on technology became even more acute. My colleague sat in the cubicle right next to mine, but we didn't communicate face-to-face at all. We messaged each other all the time: *How about lunch? Can you help me with this? How's the project going?* Emoticons flew all day long with nary a spoken word between us.

Ironically, the years of communicating in this way made us much less comfortable communicating face-to-face. We realized that we didn't really have anything to say to each other in person. Without the screens and the emojis, we'd lost the art of communication. Finally, we made a pact to look each other in the eye to communicate from then on.

My clients often grumble good-naturedly about my request that there are no laptop computers open when we're in group sessions. I believe that if there are screens present, they become a distraction. If we're all busily typing away (even if taking notes), we're not able to really connect. Human connection is the real power of coaching, and it's the beauty of our relationships with colleagues, employees, family, and friends.

A NEW, STRESSFUL REALITY

As the world becomes more technology-driven, the lines between work and home are increasingly blurred. Despite all the incredible advances that technology offers us, the efficiencies we benefit from can be a double-edged sword, driving expectations of always being "on" and filling our days with endless streams of information that we're incapable of absorbing.

We can connect with friends and family around the world with the touch of a button. We can also fall into the trap of endless social comparison via social-media posts that show us only the best parts of other people's lives. We start to feel inadequate and unsatisfied as we compare ourselves to others. We can capture the beauty of our world in high definition and share it with someone on the other side of the globe. We also risk becoming narcissistic as the selfie era spawns an entirely new form of self-obsession. This changing environment has made us dependent on communicating through a screen as we try to keep up with it all. And it feels like this new connected reality is making it that much more difficult for us to deal with stress—because all we're doing is compounding it by adding all these distractions.

Digital transformation is shifting the business landscape at an unprecedented pace. Every industry is under pressure to transform to keep up with shifting customer expectations. Add to this the increased competition for market share, and you have an environment that is challenging to navigate. Information overload is becoming a productivity killer. We are exposed to unprecedented amounts of data to help us make better decisions, but it's hard to tell the good data from the bad. We can read email, send instant messages, and surf the web while attending a conference call, but we cannot give enough attention to any one thing to truly be effective. As we try to adapt to a changing environ-

AS WE TRY TO ADAPT TO A CHANGING ENVIRONMENT, CONSTANTLY SHIFTING THE FOCUS OF OUR ATTENTION TO THE NEXT TASK, ALL OF THIS LEAVES US FEELING MORE DISCONNECTED, MORE TIME DEPRIVED, AND MORE STRESSED.

ment, constantly shifting the focus of our attention to the next task, all of this leaves us feeling more disconnected, more time deprived, and more stressed:

- According to a 2010 Science Institutes International study, 80 percent of employees find their workplace stressful, with 42 percent leaving a position solely due to stress.

- In the US alone in 2012, 280 million workdays were lost due to stress.

- According to the American Academy of Family Physicians, 75 to 90 percent of all office visits to health professionals are for stress-related symptoms and disorders.

- Stress-related illness costs the US over $1.1 trillion each year.

Leaders are no less stressed. They are faced with having to motivate and inspire employees in new ways to retain talent in a highly competitive marketplace, all while flawlessly navigating the continuous stream of email, blogs, websites, and tweets that threaten to take over every minute of the day. Success in this digital economy takes a new level of engagement, reconnecting at a very human level, and paying attention to the real conversation behind every interaction.

ENGAGEMENT, MEANING, AND PERSPECTIVE

Retaining and engaging employees in a competitive market demands a new approach, one that helps them find meaning in their work. Engagement is the cognitive, emotional, and behavioral relationship people have with their jobs, co-workers, and organizations. It is the discretionary effort and enthusiasm they put into their daily work (job satisfaction, work motivation, and organizational commitment).

Employees look for strong leadership, effective communication, and a keen awareness of the goals of the group. Leaders who provide a calm perspective on change can create a sense of meaning in the work that employees do every day. They build a shared sense of purpose that their teams can unite behind. Calm leaders are more likely to help their teams be resilient, and resilient employees see work as a source of both satisfaction and meaning in their lives.

For millennials in particular, roles that are seen as impactful are those that are connected to a higher purpose; one clearly aligned with the organization's values and vision. According to Pew Research Center, one in three business professionals are millennials, making them the largest generation in the US workforce, expected to reach seventy-five million in the future.[5] The work they do is meaningful to this demographic—when their leaders help them see the connection between what they do and the success of the organization. Leaders who communicate their expectations and goals clearly are able to align the team with those expectations. These leaders trust their employees with enough of the company's strategy to enable them to translate it to their own work and feel they're contributing to what's important for the company.

Research clearly shows the significant impact of a shared vision or core ideology on long-term financial performance. Visionary leaders are those who can see future trends and plan accordingly. But a plan alone is not enough. Successful leaders make sure every employee feels like an insider in the company, is privy to important business information, and is regularly asked for input and ideas. As Ken Blanchard writes in his book *Leading at a Higher Level,* "An

---

5   Richard Fry, "Millennials are the largest generation in the U.S. labor force," Pew Research Center, April 11, 2018, http://www.pewresearch.org/fact-tank/2018/04/11/millennials-largest-generation-us-labor-force/.

essential characteristic of great leaders is their ability to mobilize people around a shared vision." These leaders bring others along on the journey. When employees are treated like critical team members, they invariably rise to the occasion. It takes leaders who are willing to put their faith in the ability of their teams.

STUPID RATS AND THE PYGMALION EFFECT

In interactions with others, we often limit ourselves to restricted perceptions based on our own biases and stereotypes. Cognitive rigidity is when we are unable to consider alternatives to the current situation, different viewpoints, or innovative solutions to a problem. And we all suffer from it occasionally, particularly in emotionally charged situations.

Experienced leaders have an uncanny ability to detect strong performers versus poor ones and can often predict strong performance with amazing accuracy and speed. The downside to this ability is that those same leaders often fall victim to stereotyping poor performers as incapable of any improvement. Whether we realize it or not, we all make these quick judgements about someone else's ability or potential. Good or bad, these expectations affect how we interact with every member of our teams and, therefore, have a major impact on our effectiveness.

Consider your inner dialogue when working with an employee who seems to lack the capacity to execute a specific task. Compare that to when you have an employee whom you perceive as naturally skilled and remarkably "coachable." How does your attitude toward them change? Our ability to impact an employee's performance shifts based on our preconceived expectations about their skill level and capacity to learn. When we expect certain behaviors of others, we are likely to act in ways that make the expected behavior more likely to occur, in an ironically self-fulfilling-prophecy kind of way.

In 1968, Harvard researcher and psychologist, Bob Rosenthal, conducted a study in which he challenged test subjects to coach a rat through a maze. Some subjects had the easy task—half of the group were told they received extremely intelligent rats, bred and trained specifically to develop superior maze-solving skills. The other half were not so fortunate; they were informed that the rats they would be coaching through the maze were, to put it bluntly, "stupid."

In reality, they were all given plain old lab rats with no discernible differences in any of them—they were, in fact, genetically engineered to be identical, down to the last chromosome. The "smart" rats were no more skilled at maze-solving than those receiving the dubious distinction of "stupid," but the results of the experiment demonstrated the strong effect of a self-fulfilling prophecy resulting from the expectations of the coaches. The "smart" rats outperformed the "stupid" maze runners by a wide margin. It turns out the way the rats were expected to perform was exactly the way they were coached to do so, and as a result, their performance met those expectations.

Rosenthal went on to expand his experiment to the classroom, where he found similar results in school children and their teachers. At the beginning of the school year, teachers were given the names of a few students who had been identified as "gifted" and likely to bloom in the upcoming semester. As predicted by the rat experiment, the students who were labelled as gifted, despite being chosen at random, ended up with higher grades and developed into more successful students with the coaching and attention given to them by the teachers. Rosenthal called this the Expectancy or Pygmalion Effect. Teachers ended up interacting with students they believed to be gifted in a way that was much more likely to lead to richer development. Their expectation delivered the results they anticipated. Imagine if every child was given this opportunity to shine.

We all make up stories about the people in our lives. For leaders, being aware of those biases becomes even more crucial. If you find yourself making up a story about someone's ability, ask yourself whether or not it's true. Assumptions can be devastating, as people will perform up or down to our expectations.

COMMUNICATE WITH CLARITY

The first of the Four Cs of Resilience is communicate. This chapter is entitled "An Invitation to Communicate Differently." Communication is a critical skill for leaders. Effective communication leads to improvements in productivity of as much as 25 percent when employees feel engaged with their work and connected to the company mission. Communication is essential to driving productivity at every level.

Effective communications can also enable others to withstand crisis and adapt to, or rebound from, extreme challenges or adversity.

THE ABSENCE OF COMMUNICATION LEADS TO SPECULATION , AND LACK OF COMMUNICATION IS OFTEN CITED AS THE NUMBER-ONE REASON FOR ANXIETY IN THE WORKPLACE.

In times of constant change, many fears can be eased through communication that points the way forward and provides a clear call to action. The absence of communication leads to speculation, and lack of communication is often cited as the number-one reason for anxiety in the workplace. Effective leaders know that communication is crucial to driving engagement, building a resilient workforce, and creating a high-performing organization.

Three key areas drive engagement: vision, values, and voice.

UNITE BEHIND THE VISION

Unite behind the vision:

Step to the front

Lead by example to foster support

Celebrate milestones

Champion your purpose

Leaders can garner support for the organization's vision by including their teams in crafting the company's value proposition, brand values, and strategy. Instead of deciding on the vision in isolation, the most important stakeholders are invited to work with them to develop it. If they have a say in building the vision, your employees will get behind it every step of the way. And you can trust them to bring it to life.

Step to the front. Your vision is the destination toward which you are moving. Teams need to know that their leaders are as committed to the objective as they are. It can be easy to lose sight of the vision in the day-to-day running of a company. Leaders who want to keep the vision firmly in the minds of their employees will integrate it into every aspect of their communications. They stand up for it—literally in front of team members—every chance they get.

Lead by example to foster support. Having a compelling vision and trusting employees to execute on it means integrating it into every aspect of corporate life. By translating it into a methodical plan that can be embedded into every decision, every hallway conversation, and every communication becomes an opportunity to reinforce the vision. It evolves into part of the organization's everyday vernacular.

Celebrate milestones. Every accomplishment on the path to the vision, no matter how small, is a reason to celebrate. For many teams, seeing the ultimate dream become real happens over time and in incremental steps. And often we're so busy moving on to the next challenge when we finish one project that we forget to stop and celebrate the accomplishment. Pausing to reflect and celebrate the small successes keeps people engaged as they feel real progress along the way. Make every step on the journey count.

Champion your purpose. Every company has a story. If employees can see a connection between the work they do and a higher purpose, they will likely feel more engaged. Connecting their work to a greater purpose lets employees see how what they do positively impacts people and/or the planet. Employee engagement is directly linked with understanding how they are contributing to the larger mission to make a difference. This understanding leads to greater alignment with the goals of the organization. As Ken Blanchard says, "Connect the dots between individual roles and the goals of the organization. When people see that connection, they get a lot of energy out of work. They feel the importance, dignity, and meaning in their job."

DEMONSTRATE YOUR VALUES

TRUTH AND TRUST GO HAND IN HAND. Truth and trust go hand in hand. Ethics are our sense of right and wrong. The morals and values that define who we are as people are our personal ethics. How we behave in a professional setting are our professional ethics. If the two are not aligned, it creates internal conflict.

The initial belief that our values are aligned with that of a corporation, only to discover to the detriment of both our belief system and our core ethics that this is not the case, is a heartbreakingly familiar story to many. In situations where individuals are miserable and constantly fearful of losing their jobs (in extreme cases) or of making a bad decision (in many cases), creativity suffers, productivity declines, and the culture becomes toxic.

Demonstrate your values:

Be clear about your values
Be consistent through the good times and the bad

Be clear about your values. Leaders are expected to consistently demonstrate the values espoused by the organization. Employees will watch carefully for any signs that this is not the case. More than just a list of words posted in the lunchroom, values should be an integral part of the company culture, built into hiring and onboarding practices. A major American airline has seen significant success applying this practice, hiring only friendly, warm, enthusiastic people who align with their values. Executives are expected to lead by example and to trust their teams to do what's right for their customers. Employees are held accountable for upholding the values every day, and they in turn hold their leaders accountable to do the same.

Be consistent through the good times and the bad. When things are going well, it's easy to be aligned and congruent with our values. When difficulties arise, it becomes more challenging to stay the course. A deep level of self-awareness helps leaders to recognize ineffective behaviors when they do happen and to take purposeful action to re-align with their values. By demonstrating consistency during the tough times, these leaders become trustworthy.

LISTEN TO THE VOICE OF THE TEAM

We look for connections that make us feel a part of something bigger. We want to be recognized, acknowledged, and feel as though we fit in. This sense of belonging to a common cause or campaign is reinforced by communication, connecting us with others. Leaders can create connected networks and then harness the power of those communities to feel the pulse of their business. By encouraging accountability across the organization for constant improvement, every team member becomes responsible for delivering results. This sense of responsibility empowers them to drive solutions and deliver value for customers in innovative ways.

Gathering actionable feedback from employees and following up on this feedback—either in changing aspects of the process or system under review or articulating the reasons for not changing it—gives people a sense of transparency and creates a leadership team that shows both empathy and humility. Employees feel that they have been heard and that they have a seat at the table, and a voice. Follow-up and communication around decisions that have taken employee feedback into account (even if the end result is not what they were hoping for) connects employees at a deeper level with the organization. Key to this connection is creating effective feedback loops.

What do you think?

Having effective feedback loops for employees enables leaders to harness the collective wisdom of the individuals doing the work every day. Marriott International manages more than twenty brands and 3,900 properties in seventy-two countries. It employs more than 325,000 people around the world. Bill Marriott became president in November 1964 and CEO in 1972. Currently serving as chairman of the board, Marriott emphasizes how vital two-way communication is in keeping his employees fully engaged, "Every morning we have departmental standup meetings at our hotels. We'll identify the 'theme of the day': What needs work? Where are we slipping a little? Then it's all hands on deck to work on improving those areas."

Because employee input is so highly valued within the Marriott properties, these meetings always end with a simple but profound question that managers ask their employees, "What tools do you need to get your work done or to do your job more effectively?" Ensuring that all employees feel their opinions are valued and taken seriously is critical to the company's success. In his blog, Marriott says the phrase that is key to great leadership is, "What do you think?"[6] He sees it as an opportunity to allow others to express their opinions, show interest in those opinions, and demonstrate that you are willing to pursue their ideas if they have merit.

Marriott learned the phrase from President Eisenhower, and it became a powerful tool for his business. He writes, "I think that's how Eisenhower got along with all those people he had to deal with during the Second World War as a general. He had to deal with Patton, Stalin, and Roosevelt, and with Marshall, Churchill, De Gaulle, and crazy Montgomery. They were a real bunch of characters. Ike got through it all and led us to victory. Because I'm sure a lot of times he asked that question "What do you think?" He didn't necessarily do what they told him to do, but they knew he was interested in what they had to say."

Listen to the voice of the team:

Embrace diverse perspectives

Ask for feedback and mean it

Embrace diverse perspectives. Leaders have a powerful opportunity to leverage their greatest asset: people. By making the most of

---

6   Bill Marriott, "What do You Think?," Marriott on the Move, February 19, 2012, http://www.blogs.marriott.com/marriott-on-the-move/2014/02/what-do-you-think.html.

diverse talent that has a rich set of expertise, experience, and cultural backgrounds, leaders are better placed to serve a global customer base. Beyond creating a climate of inclusion, these efforts help leaders build a resilient and resourceful organization that is open to new perspectives. The greater-than-the-sum-of-our-parts concept applies if all the talent and energy of the employees in the company is engaged to the profit of the enterprise and to the creation of a healthy and dynamic corporate culture.

Ask for feedback and mean it. Great leaders listen and evaluate before making decisions. By asking what others are thinking, and in which direction they think an organization should go, leaders invite their teams to think about the business as their own. This sense of ownership and accountability is strengthened when their opinions count.

THREE CALLS TO ACTION

1. Disconnect from the screen. Take the time to connect with others in person. You'll build stronger relationships and trust.

2. Catch those assumptions. Be aware of how your perception of others could be influencing the way you interact with them.

3. Bring others along as you craft your vision, values, and purpose. Communicate them often and reinforce consistently.

CHAPTER 3

COMING THROUGH
LOUD AND CLEAR

The single biggest problem in communication is
the illusion that it has taken place.
—George Bernard Shaw

It's halfway through a talk on resilience that I am giving to an audience of over 1,000 communications leaders in Seattle. I invite an audience member up on stage and explain that I would like her to summarize—in less than two minutes—her current role and a challenge she is facing in that role. I ask that she then summarize a prior role and a challenge specific to that role, also in less than two minutes.

As she starts to speak, I am attentive, maintaining eye contact, nodding in acknowledgement, and occasionally making small noises of encouragement. My volunteer completes the first part of the exercise feeling confident in her ability to effectively engage and communicate with me. When she switches to telling me about role number two, however, I suddenly become completely consumed by something on my phone, I shift around in my chair, I break eye contact and appear mildly bored. She starts to fumble, stumbling over her words, pausing and losing her train of thought. At this point I nod and encourage her to continue her story before glancing down at my phone again as she valiantly tries to finish. This produces remarkable results. An obviously articulate, well-spoken person becomes incapacitated by nothing more than my lack of attention to what she is saying, ultimately becoming so frustrated that she stops talking entirely.

AN OBVIOUSLY ARTICULATE, WELL-SPOKEN PERSON BECOMES INCAPACITATED BY NOTHING MORE THAN MY LACK OF ATTENTION TO WHAT SHE IS SAYING.

This demonstration of the power of micromessaging to undermine performance is of course extreme. We encounter much milder forms of these types of semiconscious signals all the time—signals that we are somehow less important or interesting than someone or something else. If you have ever been in line at a store, only to be forced to wait while the clerk prioritizes a phone call over serving you, you know the feeling. Despite knowing that it is merely a demonstration, volunteers at my keynotes never fail to fall prey to the signal that they are not at all interesting. The visceral reaction to my fake microaggressions is always very real. Imagine how they would feel if this was happening to them in real life.

MIND THE (COMMUNICATION) GAP

It takes us seven seconds to assess another person based on our first impressions. In a typical ten-minute conversation, 40 to 150 micromessages are exchanged between two people. Micromessages are the subtle things we say or do that reveal infinitely more about what we think and feel than the language that we use.[7]

---

7   Mary Rowe, "Micro-affirmations & Micro-inequities," *Journal of the International Ombudsman Association* 1, no. 1 (March 2008), https://ombud.mit.edu/sites/default/files/documents/micro-affirm-ineq.pdf.

- They are subtle, semiconscious signals that can reveal a great deal about our assumptions about others.

- They are global in nature, interpreted the same way across cultures and geographies.

MICROMESSAGES ARE THE SUBTLE THINGS WE SAY OR DO THAT REVEAL INFINITELY MORE ABOUT WHAT WE THINK AND FEEL THAN THE LANGUAGE THAT WE USE.

- In the majority of cases, they are unintentional, but can still be highly impactful.

- They can reveal our core feelings or biases, creating a filter through which our communication flows.

- As we saw from my simple demonstration, they can impact performance significantly.

While unconscious, micromessaging often reveals who leaders are more connected to in the workplace. I could come into the office in the morning, greet you, and do all the right things: shake your hand and say, "Good morning Bob, how are you? How is the project coming along? Good. If you need my help, I'll be in my office. It's good to see you."

Before heading to my office, however, I take a couple of steps to the right to greet one of your colleagues, Sandy. You see me lean back, tilt my head, smile, open my arms and say, "Hey Sandy, what's going on? It's so great to see you! Let's get together later and you can get me caught up on your latest project—you're doing an amazing job!"

I have of course, been completely professional and courteous to you. But you immediately know that Sandy and I are connected in a way that you and I are not. It's not a case of you wanting to be treated the same as Sandy, but you certainly realize that you are not being treated equitably. Sandy is clearly more in favor with me.

Leaders can't be expected to treat every person the same. Personalities differ, as do communication styles, and each relationship will have an influence on the interaction. A leader may slap one colleague on the back and talk about the football score, whereas that may not be appropriate for another colleague. In the workplace context, treating people fairly means treating everyone equitably, basing business decisions on facts, and minimizing unconscious bias in the decision-making process.

THE MYSTERY OF MICROINEQUITIES

Micromessages are also called microinequities. But before we all start to see these in every interaction, a word of caution: intent to corral unintended microinequities can lead to an overwhelming sense that we can't even think without being biased. It's only a microinequity if it *doesn't* happen to everyone. If I keep checking my cell phone during conversations with my team—but I never do this if I'm talking to my CEO—we have a microinequity on our hands. If I am glued to my phone regardless of who I am talking to, then I'm just a jerk.

Microinequities are very subtle. We may not necessarily be able to articulate what exactly is wrong, but there is a feeling of being on the outside. I witnessed this in a business review where several junior-level employees were updating the executive team on both their progress for the first half of the year and the plan for the next six months. Rarely having an opportunity to present their work to the executive team, this was an important moment for them, and it was clear that they were nervous. In spite of this, they delivered an outstanding presentation, weaving their separate pieces together beautifully into a comprehensive picture. They delivered smoothly, as a unit. It was impressive. But almost everybody missed it.

The executive team members were tapping away on their keyboards or their phones throughout the presentation. Occasionally a speaker would be acknowledged, or a question asked, but on the whole, the team presented to the tops of people's heads. The executives weren't intentionally ignoring them; this was simply the cultural norm in the organization. Multitasking during meetings was to be expected, as the amount of effort put into presenting was rarely matched by the attention of the audience. Of course, had the CEO been the one presenting, it would have been a vastly different story.

CAN YOU HEAR ME NOW?

This multitasking microinequity is becoming pervasive in many companies. Listening is more difficult than ever in the new digital workplace, according to 64 percent of business professionals worldwide polled by Accenture in November 2014.[8] There's too much to do. There's too much information to take in. There are too many meetings. And the temptation to multitask is even more prevalent when we're not in the room with other people. What better time to catch up on email than during a conference call when no one is watching? Eight out of ten professionals admit to multitasking during conference calls. (Perhaps the other two aren't being entirely truthful.)

The irony is that we all know when someone is doing it. We've all been on the call where attendees clearly aren't paying attention. A question is asked that elicits the inevitable silence, followed by the "Sorry, the line cut out, what was the question?" response. And so, we repeat question after question in a never-ending rinse-and-repeat cycle, frustrating everyone on the call. When we do this, we do

---

8   "Accenture Research Finds Listening More Difficult
     in Today's Digital Workplace," Accenture, accessed
     January 2, 2019, https://www.accenture.com/za-en/
     company-accenture-research-listening-difficult-digital-workplace.

ourselves and others a disservice. Distractions take up valuable brain power that we need to pick up nuance in the conversation, access our creativity, and really think about what we're hearing. The time spent not paying attention is a wasted opportunity.

Wrong filter, faulty conclusion. Our attitude to others is influenced by our assumptions about them. If we're honest with ourselves, we'll ask whether the stories we're telling ourselves about them are accurate.

Performance is fragile. Leaders who unwittingly message microinequities can negatively impact the performance of highly capable people. Being aware of how we perceive and are perceived by others may help us avoid the trap of microinequities and nurture the talent around us.

Be present with people. When we engage fully with others not only are we more efficient, but we are more likely to experience breakthroughs. When nothing else is competing for our attention, we reap the benefits of human connection as we fully participate in what's happening around us.

WISDOM VERSUS KNOWLEDGE

KNOWING WHAT YOU DON'T KNOW AS A LEADER IS A POWERFUL TOOL ; IT FORCES YOU TO LOOK AROUND AT THE COMPETITION.

There is a saying that knowledge is knowing that a tomato is a fruit. Wisdom is not putting it into a fruit salad.

Successful CEOs are those who are constantly asking what knowledge they need to solve problems, what information they are missing, and what they can learn to help their teams succeed. Knowing what you don't know as a leader is a powerful tool; it forces you to look around at the competition. What are others doing? How are they making something work? What are they doing differently that I could copy or learn from or improve upon? Effective leaders don't assume they have all the right answers but instead focus on asking the right questions. This learner mind-set is rooted in humility, and it is key to informed decision-making.

Phil was a senior engineer who had been with the company for many years. He had seen teams, leaders, and projects come and go, and he was extremely technically proficient as well as politically astute. Affectionately known as the Oracle, I realized why he had been given this nickname when I saw him in action.

In the middle of a heated debate about a new program, Phil quietly asked a question that made us think differently about the program. He asked *why*. He wanted to gain a greater understanding of the objectives of the program—even though we were already talking about tactical execution. He shifted us to a strategic level to consider outcomes, and then he asked why we wanted to execute in a certain way when we had not stopped to consider alternatives. Phil did this frequently. He asked thoughtful questions, and he was always curious. He asked *why* more often than he asked *how*. He never critiqued or criticized any idea, instead probing gently to make sure we had thought it through, and always with a smile. He helped us get clear on what we were planning, and his humble style of communication masterfully avoided a defensive response to his suggestions. His guidance helped us run programs that had a 98 percent satisfaction rating with our customers for seven years running. By simply asking why, Phil opened us up to the possibility that there might be a better way. This was the reason he was treasured by his colleagues, respected by his peers, and beloved by my team. Phil really was our Oracle, and we were lucky to have him.

In the United States in Punxsutawney, Pennsylvania, on February 2 each year, a weather-forecasting groundhog predicts when spring is coming. Depending on whether the groundhog spots his shadow or not, the country either braces for six more weeks of winter or an early spring. Coincidentally, this most famous (and hairiest) meteorologist and oracle of weather is also named Phil.

Be like the Oracle:

Ask the right questions

Constantly be curious

Ask the right questions. Aaron Baker writes in *Heir to the Throne*: "When I think I have the right answer I ask: Why shouldn't I do it? I don't say I am going to do it and look for evidence to support my idea. I purposefully go to prove why I shouldn't do it. Don't be afraid to question your decision to make sure it's right." It's not always easy to ask the difficult questions—but the right one may change the outcome for the better.

Constantly be curious. Einstein said: "I have no special talent, I am only passionately curious." In a constantly shifting environment, lifelong learners are well equipped to deal with change. A culture of curiosity begins with leaders who are willing to listen to alternate points of view and who are willing to admit that they don't have all the answers. Employees are motivated to increase their own knowledge and contribute to the collective wisdom of the company—provided the leader sets the example.

EMBRACE EPIC FAILURE

One of the best ways to encourage employees to constantly learn and grow is to foster a culture that embraces innovation and risk-taking. A culture that is open to mistakes—and allows space to reflect on those mistakes and learn from them—creates a value system around learning. Opening our minds up to the possibilities of change exposes us to a world full of new skills, new opportunities, and new achievements. Demonstrating a high tolerance for mistakes encourages teams to be creative and innovate to solve problems. They experience mistakes as a part of learning, rather than punishment. This enables them to feel safe asking for help when missteps happen. The key is communicating this tolerance for error authentically.

Fairly early in my career as a manager I was leading a team of highly talented event planners and web developers. We were working on a huge web-migration project, moving hundreds of pages into a new web environment for our customers to use to register for the multitude of events we held each month. As we were finally nearing the end of the project, our lead web developer came into my office early one morning in tears. She confessed that she had accidentally backed up over all the new content, erasing hundreds of hours of manual work. Realizing what she had done, she was terrified to say anything to the rest of the team.

I called the team together to explain the situation. "I need your help. We've lost a lot of content. We need to recreate it, and we have to do it quickly. I know it's a lot to ask." Their shoulders sagged at the thought of the task they were facing, but every one of them stepped up. No one wasted time asking questions like, "How did this happen?"—they simply solved the problem together, as a team. We divided up the content, and we had it all recreated forty-eight grueling hours later. We also discovered some mistakes we hadn't noticed the first time, which led to a much higher-quality product.

Celebrate successes and mistakes. After we completed the project, the team took some time to "celebrate" this failure. We talked about what we would do differently the next time and the valuable lessons we had learned. We celebrated the way the team had worked together in a crisis. "I can't believe you didn't all yell at me," the lead developer told us. "Anyone else would have made me feel like a failure. The support of this team when you make a mistake is amazing. I feel so lucky to be here." It was a proud moment to see the team pull together and support each other without blame during a very difficult time. Their willingness to show empathy and embrace epic failure had given them the ability to not only withstand a crisis, but to learn and grow from it.

Not succeeding is not the same as failing. We all experience successes and failures. But the only real failure is when individuals or organizations are incapable of recovering from setbacks. Thomas Edison said, "Our greatest weakness lies in giving up. The most certain way to succeed is always to try just one more time." By creating a culture that is tolerant of mistakes, teams feel safe taking risks and innovating. When things inevitably go wrong, embracing the opportunity to learn from the experience creates a culture that is both agile and adaptable to change.

THREE CALLS TO ACTION

1. Clear the signal. Fairness does not mean treating everyone equally, but it does mean treating everyone equitably. Leaders who do so authentically build stronger relationships and show that they can be trusted.

2. Be curious. A habit of questioning the status quo is the antithesis of complacency. Leaders who do this well assume they don't have all the answers. Instead, they focus on asking the right questions.

3. Mine for the gold in mistakes. It takes conscious effort to fix mistakes when they happen without being tempted to assign blame. They often provide unforeseen insights, provided teams take the time to really learn from them.

COMMUNICATE

PART I KEY TAKEAWAYS

Plato said: "Wise men speak because they have something to say. Fools because they have to say something." Communication is key to effective engagement and must be used wisely.

Ralph Waldo Emerson said: "Do not go where the path may lead; go instead where there is no path, and leave a trail." Being willing to challenge the way things have always been done and try a new approach can reveal unforeseen opportunities.

Winston Churchill said: "Success is not final. Failure is not fatal. It's the courage to continue that counts." Leaders who demonstrate both empathy and tenacity in turbulent times garner respect and trust.

Thomas Jefferson said: "Honesty is the first chapter in the book of wisdom." Willingness to admit to not having all the answers and ask for help cultivates a humble mind-set that is adaptable to change.

PART II

BE COURAGEOUS IN TURBULENT TIMES, CHALLENGING ASSUMPTIONS, AND CHOOSING OPTIMISM

CHAPTER 4

COURAGE IN TIMES OF CHANGE

Persistence and resilience only come from having been given
the chance to work through difficult problems.
—*Gever Tulley*

In her book *Executive Presence: The Missing Link Between Merit and Success*, Sylvia Ann Hewlett describes gravitas as a core characteristic of executive presence, which she defines as "an amalgam of qualities that true leaders exude, a presence that telegraphs you're in charge or deserve to be."

Our titles at work mean very little. We earn respect every day by the way we behave. How leaders act and carry themselves reassures and inspires those around them. Employees take their cues from the leaders they work with, as their behavior becomes part of the culture of the organization. Teams follow leaders who can galvanize, energize, and inspire them. And leaders with executive presence garner respect through consistent behaviors, particularly in times of difficulty. That's when employees will want a leader who shows courage, and they will be looking for signs of incongruence.

COURAGE IN TOUGH TIMES

Strong leaders fundamentally believe in creating a culture that is adaptable and open to change. And they're not afraid to question the status quo when things get challenging. This takes a courageous mind-set. When Anders Knutsen assumed leadership of Bang & Olufsen, the Danish audiovisual company, in 1992, the business was in a state of crisis. Knutsen brought back a tradition of immaculate design and engineering, turning the company into a thriving business. His focus on doing so without destroying the heart and soul of the company had a dramatic impact on the quality of customer service. He changed the communications strategy, realizing that communication is just as important as products. His approach enabled customers across national borders to share a universal language.[9]

Knutsen got rid of the old-fashioned bureaucracy that had caused the organization to stagnate, reevaluating relationships with partners, dealers, franchisees, subsidiaries, and stakeholders. He asked everyone to come up with ideas to rationalize and save money in their areas. Employees were asked to solve the endemic problems of waste and inefficiency plaguing the organization. Knutsen put his trust in his people, and as a result, they became more accountable. They were given responsibility to improve the situation, and they stepped up to the challenge. As a result of the feedback, ideas, and input from his team, Knutsen increased efficiencies and turned a deficit of $135 million into a surplus of $270 million. He became known as the turnaround artist, renowned for his forthright management style and his tenacity in the face of adversity.

Challenge the norm. Knutsen removed hierarchy that was not effective, broke down routines that were no longer serving the

---

9   Per Thygesen Poulsen, *Anders Knutsen and Bang & Olufsen* (Centrum, 1997).

company, and was open with the press about the problems faced by the organization. Knutsen knew that the old way of doing things was no longer working. He asked for help, appealing to his employees to come up with innovative ideas to solve the problems they were facing. Tapping into the collective wisdom of his team and then acting on their input showed them that their opinions were valued. Letting go of the old ways of doing things opened the company up to creativity and innovation. Being honest about the situation built respect.

Say it in public. When a reduction in force was inevitable, Knutsen was transparent and open with employees, showing respect and appreciation for their contributions to the company. It was to his credit that he personally took care of this communication. This took the edge off critics during the two days when 290 employees were let go. Knutsen traveled to each department and told people in a straightforward way what was going to happen. In his book, *Break-point: Anders Knutsen and Bang & Olufsen*, Per Thygesen Poulsen describes Knutsen's forthright approach, "Our choice is not about firing 100 or 700 employees," he said. "It is about catastrophe or success." He even went so far to stand on a pallet in the factory and talk to the night shift of seventeen people. "If they can work in shifts, I can too." As a result, he was able to dismiss 25 percent of his workforce without strikes or criticism. When a difficult message had to be delivered, doing so openly and with respect made it easier to receive it.

Leaders who are true not only to others but to themselves are not afraid to show who they are and what matters to them. Making the tough decisions takes courage of conviction and a strong belief in our choices. Leaders who can hold steadfast to a goal during the tough times show others that they're willing to fight for what they believe in.

SHOW UP WHEN NO ONE IS WATCHING

Being in a leadership position demands a high level of integrity. Leaders are entrusted with the livelihoods and well-being of the employees who look to them to exemplify the values of the organization. Inevitably, leaders will make some bad decisions or mistakes that will call their integrity into question. Taking full responsibility for those decisions takes humility, authenticity, and courage.

When Satya Nadella, CEO of Microsoft, was asked at the Grace Hopper conference what advice he had for women who were uncomfortable asking for a pay raise or career advancement, Nadella suggested that women shouldn't ask for a raise. Given the gender pay disparity in the US high-tech industry at the time, Nadella advising women to embrace their innate confidence and have faith in the system and karma to deliver was controversial. Confounded by this response, 7,500 predominantly female engineers from around the world voiced their frustrations on social media.

Nadella immediately issued a statement to employees apologizing for his ill-conceived remarks. He said that he was "completely wrong" and that he had "learned a valuable lesson." He followed this up with an employee meeting where he took responsibility for his statement without excuses. He clearly outlined his expectations that the company would encourage and support women in advancing their careers. His authenticity, accountability, and humility won him a great deal of respect, restoring the faith of his employees and his popularity as CEO.

Fred Kiel quantified a leader's integrity in a seven-year study for his book, *Return on Character*. His study showed that CEOs rated as high-integrity leaders by employees have a direct influence on company performance:

- High-integrity CEOs = **9.4 percent** return

- Low-integrity CEOs = **1.9 percent** return

- Employee engagement is **26 percent** higher with high-integrity CEOs.

Kiel describes high-integrity CEOs this way: "They were often humble. They appeared to have very little concern for their career success or their compensation. The funny point about that is they all did better than the self-focused CEOs with regard to compensation and career success. It's sort of ironic."[10]

Take accountability. Focus on driving results is important, but effective leaders know that how you go about doing so is far more critical to success. Those who are open about their mistakes and who apologize and make amends are not perceived as less capable. Rather, they are seen as human, approachable, and trustworthy.

Do what you say you will do. By following through on their commitments, no matter how onerous, leaders who show their teams that they can be counted on are seen as trusted entities. In her book *Dare to Lead*, Brene Brown defines integrity as "choosing courage over comfort; choosing what's right over what's fun, fast, or easy; and practicing your values, not just professing them." Leaders who can be relied upon are seen as authentic.

Strength is defined as optimism, decisive action, perseverance, and taking responsibility. Honor is defined as integrity, ethical behavior, and open communication. Leaders who take responsibility for their actions and have the courage to admit when they are wrong are seen as having high integrity. Those who do so with humility are seen as strong.

---

10 Fred Kiel, *Return on Character: The Real Reason Leaders and Their Companies Win*, (Boston: Harvard Business Review Press, 2015).

BE AN ALLY, NOT A HERO

According to the *Harvard Business Review*, "Leaders who do undertake a voyage of personal understanding and development can transform not only their own capabilities but also those of their companies."[11]

The humble leader levels the playing field, sets ego aside and engages others in collaborative problem solving. Innovation typically requires team effort. By taking a learning rather than a knowing orientation and being curious, we become open to new ideas and give others an opportunity to contribute and shine, building trust and a sense of shared purpose and camaraderie.

THE VERY BEST THING WE CAN DO FOR ANY GROUP OR INDIVIDUAL IS TO GIVE THEM POWER OVER THEIR OWN LIVES.

The days of the hero leading the charge are over. The very best thing we can do for any group or individual is to give them power over their own lives. When leaders fail to do this, we rob others of their self-esteem and their capability. If we constantly step in and do for others what they are capable of doing for themselves, we enslave them, taking away their self-worth and making them dependent on us for every decision.[12]

This lesson was brought home to me when I returned to visit a small team that I had led for about four years. I had left the team in the capable hands of my most senior team member, Veronica, a quietly efficient, well-respected individual who had the experience, the ability, and the intimate knowledge of the organization to succeed. When I

---

11   David Rooke and William R. Torbert, "Seven Transformations of Leadership," *Harvard Business Review*, April 2005, https://hbr.org/2005/04/seven-transformations-of-leadership.

12   Ivy Gutierrez, "Micromanagement – What is it and How to do it Well," Swipetrack Solutions, 2017, http://blog.swipetrack.com/micromanagement-do-it-well/.

met with my ex-manager a month later, I asked how the team was doing. "You cast a very wide shadow," he said. He expressed concerns about the new leader's confidence and ability to manage the team. I felt terrible. Had my approach of stepping in and doing for others rather than holding them accountable and empowering them to do for themselves robbed Veronica of her confidence? I had not respected her ability to deliver. Instead, any time we encountered an obstacle, I had stepped in to be the hero, clearly at her expense. Instead of helping (which was my selfish justification for my hero behavior), I was letting Veronica know that I would always be there to save the day, robbing her of the confidence to take on a leadership role. Despite believing that she was fully capable, I had not demonstrated this to her. Instead, I had deactivated and demotivated her. The reality of my ego-driven behavior wasn't an easy thing to face, but it was a humbling and important lesson for me. And for Veronica, no longer having a hero manager holding her back enabled her to grow more confident and she blossomed over the next few months, becoming the outstanding team leader she was always capable of being.

Get in the trenches with your team. Thomas Edison said, "If we did the things we are capable of, we would astound ourselves." The same applies to believing in the capability of others. It's a fine balance for every leader to be an ally fighting alongside their team, rather than a hero taking over for them. Showing confidence in the team's ability gives them the courage to act. By respecting their free agency and their innate right to make decisions, leaders can empower their employees to get the job done, while holding them accountable for doing so and giving them the credit when those efforts are rewarded.

Clear the obstacles and get out of the way. The real job of the leader is to set the path, align teams with the objectives, help them overcome obstacles (when needed), and then step out of the way.

Trusting others' capability to deliver and giving them the space to do so is a powerful motivational force. This takes an optimistic view of the team's ability to perform, balanced by willingness to hold that performance to the highest possible standard.

KIND LEADERSHIP IS NOT NICE LEADERSHIP

A California State Long Beach study found that leaders who treat their employees fairly have more productive and cohesive teams.[13] A key element of these leaders was their ability to be kind without being pushovers.[14]

I had been leading a small team for a few years when Martha joined us as a researcher. It wasn't long before I started hearing complaints about her communication style. Her superior, condescending tone was becoming a problem for the rest of the team, who were starting to dread being in meetings with her. It got so bad that they started calling them "Martha's lectures."

I invited Martha into my office after one such incident. "You were pretty rough on the team Martha, I'm worried about you. Are you OK?" Her eyes filled with tears. She told me that she had to fight to be heard as the only girl in a family of four older brothers. She was always in competition with them to see who was smarter. It was one of the reasons she had earned a PhD and why she always needed to be the one who had all the answers. I handed her a tissue. "Martha, we

---

13   Elad N. Sherf, Ravi S. Gajendran, and Vijaya Venkataramani, "Research: When Managers Are Overworked, They Treat Employees Less Fairly," *Harvard Business Review*, June 4, 2018, https://hbr.org/2018/06/research-when-managers-are-overworked-they-treat-employees-less-fairly.

14   Jason A. Colquitt, et al., "Justice at the millennium, a decade later: A meta-analytic test of social exchange and affect-based perspectives," *Journal of Applied Psychology 98, no. 2* (2013): 199-236, http://psycnet.apa.org/doi/10.1037/a0031757.

all know you're intelligent. You have a PhD, you're great at what you do, and you are highly articulate. It's why we hired you in the first place. But you're coming across as a lecturing professor rather than a part of the team. I need you to stop talking down to your colleagues and start collaborating with them. If you can't do that, then you have no place on this team."

After a few minutes of stunned silence, she surprised me by nodding. "You're right. I've been trying so hard to be the most competent person in the room that I didn't realize how I was coming across. I'm going to be better." Martha did change. She worked well with the team, and her attitude improved so much she became one of the most respected people in our organization. A few months later Martha told me, "When I first met you, you were so nice I thought you'd be a pushover," she laughed. "I learned the hard way that you may be kind, but that doesn't make you weak."

Be kind, not cowardly. Giving feedback isn't always easy, and it's particularly difficult when the feedback is perceived as negative. But telling people the truth they need to hear is an act of kindness. Protecting them and ourselves from a difficult conversation is both a disservice to them—and a chickenhearted act of cowardice.

Be strong, not harsh. Strength is important for leadership. People expect courage from their leaders, or they will not follow them. But strength is not about controlling behavior or being a bully. Leaders who dominate others don't inspire loyalty, particularly when

KINDNESS IS GUIDING YOUR TEAM TO LEARN AND GROW. RESPECT IS HOLDING THEM ACCOUNTABLE FOR IMPROVEMENT.

delivering feedback. Setting emotions aside and delivering accurate and objective feedback that considers the feelings and perspective of the employee enables them to receive it without becoming defensive.

Kindness is guiding your team to learn and grow. Respect is holding them accountable for improvement.

NAVIGATING THE HUMAN SIDE OF CHANGE

Every aspect of life involves some form of transition. The Transition Model was created by change-consultant, William Bridges, and was published in his 1991 book *Managing Transitions*. The main strength of the model is that it focuses on transition, not change. The difference between these is subtle but important.

Transition is the inner psychological process that we go through as we internalize and come to terms with the new situation that change brings about. The starting point for dealing with transition is not the outcome, but the endings that we must deal with as we leave the old situation behind.

Change is situational. It is the external event that is taking place which is perceived as an ending—loss of a loved one, divorce, moving to another place, loss of a job, or retirement. In business, it could be a new strategy, a change in leadership, layoffs, a merger, or a new policy or product. Organizations naturally focus on the outcome that the change will produce, which is usually in response to external pressures. But the key to any change being successful is moving people through the transition.

There are three phases of transition:

Letting go

Entering the neutral zone

Accepting a new beginning

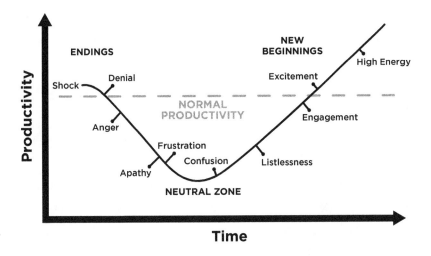

1. Letting go

Every transition starts with an ending. My team had created an annual event that we were all enormously proud of. It was the most important event of the year for our audience of technical partners—when we would announce the winners of our annual awards. The event was a lavish, three-day affair in a beautiful location that included Microsoft's co-founder, Bill Gates, and the then-CEO of Microsoft, Steve Ballmer, on stage along with various industry luminaries, all sharing technical breakthroughs and inspirational stories with the six hundred-person audience of technical partners and their guests. All of this culminated in a glittering awards ceremony where the winners of the prestigious awards were revealed.

When the economic downturn of 2008 happened, Microsoft instituted a massive reduction in force. Our team was fortunate not to be affected by those layoffs, but we were informed that our event was being canceled. The team was crushed. They had worked on this event for three years in a row, and it was both highly anticipated and enormously valuable for our partners. We'd put everything we had into making the event spectacular. Of course, we understood that the cost of the event was no longer sustainable given the economic situation, but it was still a bitter pill to swallow. It was an ending that we would have to come to terms with.

The first phase of any transition begins when people identify what they are losing and learn how to manage these losses. The loss may be perceived as the end of an era. They move through the process of determining what is over and being left behind, and what they will keep as they move forward. This may include relationships, systems, processes, locations, or team members. In our case, it was both the end of a landmark event, and of a time when we had the freedom to innovate and be creative at almost any cost.

2. Entering the neutral zone

The neutral zone is a place of growth. A few days after we got the news, one of the team members suggested that we have a "wake" to mourn the loss of the event. We gathered to share funny memories and put the past behind us. Interestingly, it was during this conversation that ideas came up for alternative formats for the event. The team developed a format that would be much more cost-effective but still deliver the recognition that our partners were deserving of. Pausing to grieve allowed us to let go of the old event and to find our creativity and innovate in a new direction.

When we enter the neutral zone, we go through an in-between time when the old is gone but the new isn't yet fully operational. This is when psychological realignments take place to enable us to embrace a new beginning. It is the very core of the transition process. This is the time between the old reality and sense of identity and the new one.

Teams in this stage are creating new processes and learning what their roles in the new reality will be. It is in the neutral zone that acceptance of the new reality and growth occur. Acceptance is not apathy or

resignation. It is the beginning of new possibilities. For my team, this was the space we
needed to incubate new ideas. Embracing
the "grieving" period in the neutral zone
gave us an opportunity to start to see the
possibilities in the new beginning.

> ACCEPTANCE IS
> NOT APATHY OR
> RESIGNATION. IT IS
> THE BEGINNING OF
> NEW POSSIBILITIES.

3. Accepting a new beginning

Embarking on a new beginning brings energy. Together we presented
the plan for the new event format to our leadership, and they loved
it. We scaled the event down to a single evening with only the award
nominees and their guests attending. The new, more intimate format
was very well received, in no small part because it represented an
organization that could innovate to deliver an incredible experience
on a tight budget.

Beginnings may involve new values and new attitudes. They are
marked by a release of energy in a new direction—often with an
expression of a fresh identity for the team or organization. A well-
managed transition allows teams to establish new roles with clarity
of purpose and an understanding of the part they play in the new
vision, including how they can contribute and participate most effectively in making it real.

Leaders who can help move their teams through the neutral
zone benefit not only from renewed energy and refreshed focus; they
can also enhance the ingenuity and resourcefulness that any new
beginning needs to succeed.

THREE CALLS TO ACTION

1. Show respect. Having faith in others' capabilities and respecting them enough to not do for them what they can do for themselves shows both respect and trust.

2. Have the courage to be honest. Being nice by not confronting an individual's bad behavior is telling that person something that's not true and is doing him or her a disservice.

3. Plans rarely match reality. Embracing the creativity of the neutral zone enables us to navigate through change and move to new beginnings.

CHAPTER 5

AN ATTITUDE OF GRATITUDE

Everything can be taken from a man but one thing:
the last of the human freedoms—
to choose one's attitude in any given set of circumstances,
to choose one's own way.
—Victor Frankl

Looking back now, Peter and I agree that the carjacking was a catalyst for a new life direction and the best thing that could have happened to us. Of course, at the time it didn't feel that way.

Collins Dictionary defines hindsight as "the ability to understand and realize something about an event after it has happened, although you did not understand or realize it at the time." Reflecting on our journey, had the carjacking not happened, it is likely that Peter and I would still be in South Africa. We would not have been exposed to the experiences we've had in the United Kingdom, nor would we have had an opportunity to live and work in the United States. And I would certainly not be serving executives and leaders in my own coaching business, an opportunity that gives me enormous joy and satisfaction.

> EVERY STEP WE HAVE TAKEN AND DECISION WE HAVE MADE SINCE WERE AS A DIRECT RESULT OF THAT SINGLE EVENT, AND TRAUMATIC THOUGH IT WAS AT THE TIME, I WILL ALWAYS BE GRATEFUL FOR THAT EXPERIENCE.

Every experience has helped us build resilience, adapt to change, and develop the determination to overcome disappointment. Without them, we would not have grown as people in the ways that we have. Every step we have taken and decision we have made since were as a direct result of that single event, and traumatic though it was at the time, I will always be grateful for that experience.

YOU CAN'T STOP THE WAVES, BUT YOU CAN LEARN TO SURF

Gratitude is a mind-set that enables us to seek out new experiences. It creates and maintains the positive attitude of the explorer in each of us. By viewing our lives as works in progress, we learn to take on greater responsibilities at work and at home and seek out experiences that will challenge us to learn more about ourselves. It also deepens our connection to others, giving us the courage to reach out, and broadening our perspective.

It's easy for unpleasant emotions to dominate our awareness. Our brains are wired to constantly scan for and identify threats. But we can train our brains to be more positive. Gratitude, through a conscious awareness and repeated focus on the good things that come our way, amplifies our appreciation of both our blessings and our benefactors. Happiness is causal, bringing more benefits than simply feeling good. Happy people have been shown to be more successful, more socially engaged, and healthier than unhappy people. Researchers studying the impact of stressors on illness discovered that people who experience a lot of positive emotions such as gratitude, love, or happiness are less likely to catch a cold or the flu than those who experience more negative emotions. Focusing on positive emotions boosts our immune system.[15, 16]

Having an attitude of gratitude does not mean never experiencing negative emotions. Negative thoughts have their place, particularly when dealing with events over which we have no control, such as natural disasters or the death of a loved one. Regardless of our thinking style, most of us would find such events extremely stressful. But the stress we feel each day rarely comes from such extremes or situations where our literal survival is determined by the quickness of our response. Consciously cultivating an attitude of gratitude helps us to avoid being overwhelmed by day-to-day stressors by training our brains to notice the positive. Keeping our gratitude higher than our expectations keeps things in perspective.[17]

One of the major literary figures in the first third of the twentieth century, G.K. Chesterton, set himself the conscious goal to remain childlike in his sense of wonder and vowed not to succumb to the monotony and boredom that saps so many lives of joy and purpose. In his autobiography, he writes: "One is never lacking in opportunities to be happy, because around every corner is another gift waiting to surprise us, and it will surprise us, if we can achieve control over our natural tendencies to make comparisons, to take things for granted and to feel entitled."

---

15   Jo Marchant, "How Happiness Boosts the Immune System," *Scientific American*, 2013, https://www.scientificamerican.com/article/how-happiness-boosts-the-immune-system/.

16   "Happiness = Health," *Research Matters*, 2009, http://www.researchmatters.ku.edu/2009/march/happy.shtml.

17   "Grateful Resilience – Day 157 – 366 Days of Resilience," Silver Lobster Ltd, 2016, https://silverlobster.wordpress.com/2016/01/01/grateful-resilience-day-157-366-days-of-resilience/.

IN PRAISE OF GRATITUDE

Gratitude can change your life for the better. A 2012 University of Kentucky study showed that intentionally noticing the good things in life and being grateful for them builds neural pathways to optimism, enhances empathy, and reduces aggression. Multiple studies have revealed a strong link between gratitude and well-being. An attitude of gratitude improves psychological health, increasing happiness and reducing depression.[18] By focusing on the good things in life, we can reduce toxic emotions like envy, resentment, frustration, and regret.

AN ATTITUDE OF GRATITUDE IMPROVES PSYCHOLOGICAL HEALTH, INCREASING HAPPINESS AND REDUCING DEPRESSION.

But gratitude is not just good for our brains. It improves our physical health, too. Positive psychology research published in *American Psychologist* shows that grateful people experience fewer aches and pains, exercise more often and have regular medical check-ups. They also sleep better. Writing in a gratitude journal fifteen minutes before bed helped them to fall asleep faster and sleep more soundly. Keeping a gratitude journal to remind us to count our blessings is a powerful way to focus on the positive aspects of life. And it's a powerful way to build a book of memories to look back on years later.

Expressing gratitude directly also gives us an instant boost of happiness. Gratitude changes the way we interact with the world and promotes thoughts that are conducive to recovery from stressful events. It requires a shift in mind-set and a new way of being. And that can be challenging given our propensity to return to a baseline

---

18   C. Nathan DeWalt, et al., "A Grateful Heart is a Nonviolent Heart," *Sage Journals* 3, no. 2 (September 6, 2011): 232-40, https://doi.org/10.1177%2F1948550611416675.

of happiness regardless of either positive or negative events. This tendency is called the hedonic treadmill.

Two psychologists, Brickman and Campbell, first described the hedonic treadmill (or hedonic adaptation) in 1971, stating that processes similar to sensory adaptation occur when people respond emotionally to different life events. They suggested that our emotional system goes back to the level prior to the event after some time. While different personality traits may predispose individuals to different levels of well-being, in her book *The How of Happiness*, researcher Sonja Lyubomirsky writes: "Your actions, thoughts, and words account for 40 percent of your happiness, which is significant." By consciously cultivating gratitude, we can short-circuit the hedonic treadmill and boost our happiness.

Contemplate the good. Focusing on the positive each day shifts our perspective. Writing them down helps us keep them in mind. Reflecting on moments of gratitude builds neural pathways to optimism, regardless of whether we naturally see the glass as half full or half empty.

Pay it forward. Random acts of kindness can dramatically improve our happiness. Stanford students who were asked to perform five random acts of kindness over a week reported much higher happiness levels than those of a control group. The acts of kindness were appreciated by the recipients, and those who were giving felt good about themselves. In his book, *Flourish*, Martin Seligman writes, "Doing a kindness produces the single most reliable momentary increase in well-being of any exercise we have tested."

A LESSON FROM THE CONVENT

In a quiet locale in New England, the convent of the School Sisters of Notre Dame on Good Counsel Hill is home to 678 Catholic nuns who have been part of a pioneering study designed to answer questions about who gets Alzheimer's, and why.

The School Sisters wrote autobiographical essays sharing their thoughts, dreams, and aspirations as they prepared to enter a life of servitude to God. These same Sisters, who toward the end of the fifteen-year study ranged in age from 75 to 106, also allowed unprecedented access to their personal and medical histories and underwent rigorous annual mental and physical testing.

A key area of focus of the study was positive emotional state early in life, evidenced in part by the autobiographical essays the nuns wrote. The differences in low and high positive emotion are clear in two examples of the autobiographies:

> Sister 1 wrote: *I was born on September 26, 1909, the eldest of seven children, five girls and two boys. My candidate year was spent in the Motherhouse, teaching chemistry and second-year Latin at Notre Dame Institute. With God's grace, I intend to do my best for our Order, for the spread of religion, and for my personal sanctification.*

> Sister 2 wrote: *God started my life off well by bestowing upon me a grace of inestimable value. The past year which I have spent as a candidate studying at Notre Dame College has been a very happy one. Now I look forward with eager joy to receiving the Holy Habit of Our Lady and to a life of union with Love Divine.*

Researchers from the University of Kentucky categorized the nun's autobiographies into four levels of positivity and compared them with how well the nuns were doing fifteen years later. The Sisters were ideal for scientific study because of their stable, relatively similar lives. They didn't smoke and hardly drank; they never had sexual intercourse, got married, or had children. They were all Caucasian women and ate in convent cafeterias, and most were teachers in Catholic schools. The only variable was the positivity of their attitude in their autobiographies and its correlation to happiness.

The findings were remarkable:

- The happiest nuns lived **ten years longer** than the least happy nuns

- By age, the happiest group had lost only **25 percent** of its population, whereas the least happy group had lost **60 percent**

- **54 percent** of the happiest nuns reached the age of ninety-four, compared with only **15 percent** of the least happy nuns.

The nun study shows an incredibly strong link between how happy we are today and how long we could live. It is also an inspiring story of remarkable women whose dedication to serving others may help all of us live longer and healthier lives. We can learn a great deal from the School Sisters about the power of positive perception.[19]

THREE AMAZING THINGS

One of my favorite perception-shifting exercises in my resilience workshops is to ask participants to write down three amazing things that happened to them that day. This is usually met with a certain degree of skepticism. On one occasion, an attendee at the back of the room responded to this request with eye-rolling and a heavy sigh. "Nothing amazing has happened to me today, just normal stuff," she muttered, giving me a look that plainly said I had lost my mind.

I asked her to describe her day so far. "Well, I woke up in my hotel room, had a shower, and had breakfast before coming here."

---

19 Pam Belluck, "Nuns Offer Clues to Alzheimer's and Aging," *The New York Times*, May 7, 2001, https://www.nytimes.com/2001/05/07/us/nuns-offer-clues-to-alzheimer-s-and-aging.html.

She shrugged. I asked if her hotel room was comfortable and had a nice bed. She confirmed it did. I asked if the shower had hot water and was restorative. She affirmed that it was so. Finally, I inquired about her breakfast, which turned out to be a cornucopia of delicious choices. As she finished cataloguing these events, I asked her to consider whether a having a nice room, a soft bed, a hot shower, and a delicious breakfast could possibly be considered amazing.

> Each heartbeat pumps 20 percent of the blood in our bodies to our brains. The harder we think, the more oxygen the brain uses. Of the 50,000 thoughts that run through our minds each day, 70 percent are negative. Imagine what we could achieve if we could focus all that brainpower on the good stuff.

At this point, the rest of the attendees started to get the idea. One by one they jumped up to share their own stories, everything from having a good night's sleep, to getting their children to school on time, to having the opportunity to sip coffee with their significant other before heading out, to a smile from a stranger. Nobody had won the lottery. There were no life-changing stories of survival or overcoming hardship. These were the stories of everyday moments. But as we started to view them through a lens of gratitude, the everyday became amazing. Not to be outdone, even our naysayer joined in, tentatively at first, and finally with gusto as she shifted her own perspective to see the extraordinary in the ordinary.

Replay the extraordinary. By writing down three amazing things every day for a week and then looking back on the list, we can shift our perspective to one of appreciating the small gifts and simple pleasures that we so often overlook. This may feel awkward at first, but persistence counts. Many people find that within a few weeks, this approach gradually moves their mind-set in a positive direction.

Share the good. Extending the appreciation of the good in life by sharing our observations with others has been known to increase happiness both for the person doing the sharing and the recipient of the message. I encourage my clients to have their families join in, sharing their lists of three amazing things at the end of each day.

FROM GRATEFUL TO GREAT

Research conducted by Globoforce found that 78 percent of employees say they work harder when their efforts are recognized and appreciated. Their research indicates a direct correlation between the frequency of recognition and the percentage of employees who feel appreciated, love their jobs, and intend to stay.[20] Treating teams well and acknowledging their efforts and contributions openly is key to engagement. In *The Future of Leadership*, Brigette Tasha Hyacinth writes: "If you don't show appreciation to those that deserve it, they'll learn to stop doing the things you appreciate."

- **65 percent** of people surveyed in a 2011 Gallup poll said they received no recognition for good work the previous year.

- **41 percent** of companies that use peer-to-peer recognition have seen marked positive increases in customer satisfaction (in 2012).

- Peer-to-peer appreciation is **35 percent** more likely to have a positive impact on financial results than manager-only recognition (according to a Globoforce Employee recognition survey in 2012).

---

20 Shweta Agarwal, "More Americans Satisfied with Recognition at Work," Globoforce, 2012, https://www.globoforce.com/press-releases/globoforce-survey-more-americans-satisfied-with-recognition-at-work/.

There's an art to the practice of appreciation, and it involves gratitude. Gratitude is about having an abundance mind-set. When we think abundantly, our perception of everything and everyone around us shifts in a positive way, and we can express appreciation authentically. The number-one reason most employees leave their jobs is that they don't feel appreciated. Nothing motivates employees more than respect and feeling valued for the work they do.

THE NUMBER-ONE REASON MOST EMPLOYEES LEAVE THEIR JOBS IS THAT THEY DON'T FEEL APPRECIATED.

One of the ways I like to start team meetings is by expressing appreciation, putting the entire team into a more open, collaborative mind-set before we start on the list of tasks we need to accomplish. I start by thanking one or two team members for something that I appreciate them doing (usually something outside of their ordinary day-to-day deliverables). We then go around the table, with each person on the team expressing appreciation for something or someone else. Although it can take a while for teams to get into the spirit of the practice, when they do, the results can be remarkable. They pause and take the time to consider just how much they mean to each other. Expressing gratitude authentically takes a degree of vulnerability, breaks down political siloes, brings teams closer together, and lets them know that they are held in high esteem.

THE BENEFIT IS IN THE
EYE OF THE BEHOLDER

It's the little gestures that make the biggest impressions. Becoming a known and trusted entity as a leader takes consistent championing of your team, from the big decisions that impact the bottom line, to the everyday interactions that define the leader you aspire to be. Appreciation is key to employee engagement and to becoming a leader who others will follow. The catch is that it has to be authentic.

An executive I worked with for several years sends handwritten welcome notes to every new employee in her organization. This tiny, personal gesture has a significant effect on teams who otherwise would never have an opportunity to interact with someone at her level. The notes open the door to engagement at a profoundly human level and create a culture where everyone feels valued, appreciated, and heard. Many of her employees write thank-you notes to the leader in return, or post photos of their welcome cards with messages of appreciation on social media. One even went so far as to write her a poem to express his gratitude for such a warm welcome.

Put it in writing. A gesture in the form of a handwritten thank-you note or even an email to let employees know how much you appreciate them goes a long way to gaining loyalty and building trust. Employees who feel appreciated and valued become ambassadors for the team and the company, and the return on that investment is immeasurable.

THREE CALLS TO ACTION

1. Find extraordinary moments. Writing down the things that make the ordinary amazing helps us focus on the positive and acts as a buffer for stress.

2. Harness the power of gratitude. Gratitude is a "moral motivator"—when teams experience gratitude, they are motivated to engage in prosocial behavior. It is also a "moral reinforcer"—when an individual expresses gratitude, it encourages their benefactors to act favorably toward them in the future.

3. Show appreciation. Small gestures of appreciation have a ripple effect, creating a culture that is profoundly personal and a workforce that is engaged and invested.

CHAPTER 6

CHOOSE OPTIMISM

*Think twice before you speak, because your words
and influence will plant the seed of either success or
failure in the mind of another.*
—Napoleon Hill

A disturbing trend in our society is to do everything in our power to avoid frustration, failure, or disappointment. Helicopter parents overprotect their children, involving themselves in their lives more as best friends than parents. Schools do away with scoring sports matches so that neither team will feel like "losers." Exuberant athletes showing too much joy when scoring are penalized for making the other team feel inadequate. At many high schools in the United States, the graduation-day tradition of crowning a valedictorian, the prestigious title that goes to the senior with the highest grade point average, is being done away with in an effort not to erode the self-esteem of the other students. Our culture is increasingly removing the healthy competition that helps each generation balance winning and losing as a normal part of life. If everyone gets a trophy simply for participating, there is no incentive to work hard and strive for more, and no desire to raise the standard at which we do anything. As we worship at the altar of self-esteem, we become a society in which individualism is becoming rampant, and more and more people believe that they are the center of the universe.

Research suggests that unwarranted high self-regard can lead to violent and criminal behavior. Instead of pushing for self-esteem, parents and educators should be teaching resilience and optimism. Studies have shown that those with an optimistic outlook are higher achievers and have better overall health.

> RESEARCH SUGGESTS THAT UNWARRANTED HIGH SELF-REGARD CAN LEAD TO VIOLENT AND CRIMINAL BEHAVIOR. INSTEAD OF PUSHING FOR SELF-ESTEEM, PARENTS AND EDUCATORS SHOULD BE TEACHING RESILIENCE AND OPTIMISM.

The American Psychological Association found that millennials in particular have higher rates of stress, depression, and suicide than any generation before them.[21] Parents and teachers can handicap children by making their lives too easy. Taught that having high self-esteem and exuding confidence is more important than persisting and overcoming obstacles, their belief that they will always succeed makes the thought of individual failure inconsolable.

When young people are accommodated and protected to the extent that they don't get to test themselves against their environment, they can have a problem growing up, making decisions, and coping with stress. When life inevitably presents them challenges, they can develop a deep-seated sense of helplessness, generalizing a particular instance of adversity into a permanent characteristic. At work, they

---

21 "Paying With Our Health, Stress in America," American Psychological Association, February 4, 2015, https://www.apa.org/news/press/releases/stress/2014/stress-report.pdf.

need instant and constant gratification and can be prone to giving up easily if the job doesn't meet their emotional needs. When things don't go the way they had hoped, they can become paralyzed and dependent, unable to cope with obstacles, and unwilling to try.

Without ever experiencing any frustration or setback and learning to overcome it, even managing minor conflicts or challenges can create stress. It is unrealistic to expect a perfect score all the time, and in life generally. Without the inner resources to motivate them to continue to move toward successful goals in the face of adversity, an entire generation is at risk of imploding.

BRICK WALLS ARE THERE FOR A REASON

When Carnegie Mellon professor Randy Pausch learned that he had terminal cancer, he decided to make his final lecture about the most important lessons he had learned in his life. In it, he emphasized that "experience is what you get when you didn't get what you wanted. And experience is often the most valuable thing you have to offer." He was clear on the need to overcome obstacles and, in doing so, learn from the experience. Brick walls, he said, are there for a reason. "Complaining does not work as a strategy. We all have finite time and energy. Any time we spend whining is unlikely to help us achieve our goals. And it won't make us happier."

Pausch also reinforces the need to be prepared for the worst. "Yes, I am a great optimist, but when trying to make a decision, I often think of the worst-case scenario. I call it the 'eaten by wolves factor.' What is the most terrible thing that could happen? Would I be eaten by wolves? One thing that makes it possible to be an optimist is if you have a contingency plan for when all hell breaks loose. There are a lot of things

I don't worry about, because I have a plan in place if they happen."[22]

A client was struggling with keeping her composure when dealing with a difficult team of stakeholders. She was so frustrated that she was thinking of leaving the team. We worked to shift her perspective from focusing on their behavior and instead prepared her for the worst-case scenario—helping her become aware of how she would be triggered by the aggressive, antagonistic behaviors of the individuals on this team, so that she was ready for it when it happened.

INSTEAD OF SHUTTING DOWN, REACTING DEFENSIVELY, OR TRYING TO SHOUT OVER THEM, SHE RESPONDED CONSTRUCTIVELY, CONFIDENTLY, AND FIRMLY.

When it did, she would take a few deep breaths and center herself before responding. If they interrupted her, she would wait patiently for them to finish and diplomatically ask that they let her convince them of her point of view. Instead of shutting down, reacting defensively, or trying to shout over them, she responded constructively, confidently, and firmly. She was resolute and unshakable, while still being flexible and approachable. Every time they attacked, she would respond in the same way, with calm assertiveness.

By focusing on how she would respond to this group, my client was prepared for the worst. Instead of fixating on the specifics of their behavior or giving up entirely, she took control of her response rather than reacting emotionally. She also shifted her perception of the relationship itself. By taking an optimistic outlook—looking at the relationship through the lens of shared objectives rather than personal outcomes—she was much more prepared to facilitate a compromise. Over time, her consistently measured approach garnered the team's

---

22 "Randy's Pausch's Last Lecture," Carnegie Mellon University, accessed January 3, 2019, https://www.cmu.edu/randyslecture/.

respect, as she made it clear that she was not willing to be bullied or to become a bully to win. She brokered a more productive relationship with her stakeholder team, moving the partnership forward by focusing on mutual goals and truly listening to their concerns.

Ultimately, both parties benefited from a shift in perspective. My client was, to use Pausch's analogy, not eaten by wolves. By being mindful of what our initial thoughts are in reacting to situations, we can focus on what we need to change to view the entire situation differently and be prepared for every eventuality. As Pausch puts it, "Luck is where preparation meets opportunity."

GETTING OVER THE WALL

Despite equal talent and drive, optimists succeed where pessimists fear to tread. Learned optimism is a term coined by psychologist Martin Seligman. Seligman explains that just like learned helplessness, optimism can be learned. Seligman and many other positive psychology studies show that people with an optimistic outlook are higher achievers and have better overall health. Unfortunately, pessimism has proven to be much more common.

JUST LIKE LEARNED HELPLESSNESS, OPTIMISM CAN BE LEARNED.

The gift hidden within the pessimistic attitude is hardheaded realism. Pessimists portray situations more accurately in a world where a tincture of pessimism might be crucial to foreseeing and thus avoiding potential disaster. But it is important to strike a balance. Those pessimists who want to maintain their more accurate picture of reality and yet reap the benefits of hopefulness should cultivate "flexible optimism," as opposed to blind optimism. The idea is to change the way you explain bad events to yourself, to offer arguments against absorbing all the personal blame for setbacks, and in doing so, limit adversity's impact on different areas of your life. You need optimism if you're trying to achieve a goal, keep your morale high, maintain a healthy immune system, or lead others.

Someone with a pessimistic explanatory style is more likely to give up in the face of adversity and to experience depression and anxiety. Seligman encourages pessimists to learn to be optimists by thinking about their reactions to adversity in a new way. The resulting optimism and change in explanatory style is what Seligman calls a "learned optimism."[23]

HALF EMPTY, HALF FULL

Explanatory style is a psychological attribute that indicates how people explain to themselves why they experience a particular event, either positive or negative. Psychologists have identified three components to explanatory style:

Three Components to Explanatory Style:

Permanence

Pervasiveness

Personalization

1. Permanence

Optimistic people tend to believe negative events to be more temporary than permanent. They recover from setbacks quickly, whereas others may take longer periods to recover or may never recover. Optimists also believe good things happen for reasons that are permanent, rather than focusing on the transient nature of

---

23 Martin E. P. Seligman, *Learned Optimism: How to Change Your Mind and Your Life* (New York: Random House, 2006).

positive events. Optimists also point to specific temporary causes for negative events; while pessimists point to permanent causes.

2. Pervasiveness

Optimistic people compartmentalize helplessness, whereas pessimistic people assume that failure in one area of life means failure in life as a whole. Optimistic people also allow good events to influence other areas of their lives rather than just the particular area in which the event occurred. Optimists also expect problems to be temporary and will isolate a troubling event and not extrapolate it into a permanent explanation, which pessimists are likely to do.

3. Personalization

Optimists tend to attribute failure to causes outside of themselves, whereas pessimists tend to blame their inability or behavior for setbacks that occur. Optimists are therefore able to process setbacks faster and generally take greater personal responsibility for a failure, seeing it as a temporary challenge rather than something that affects all areas of their lives. They challenge negative thoughts, reframe their perspective, and focus on taking action by dispassionately analyzing the accuracy of those thoughts.

A person with an optimistic outlook will perceive failure as an event that was simply unlucky and a setback or challenge, rather than a permanent or personal reflection of their ability to succeed. They know that the challenge they are so distracted by today is unlikely to make a difference in a few years. They make a conscious choice not to be trapped by circumstances.

Leaders who can imbue their teams with the understanding that pain is a temporary condition and an opportunity to learn, build an optimistic foundation in the face of adversity—a foundation on which they can reinvent the future. Looking at situations through the lens of realistic optimism builds resilience. Harnessing the power of awe makes us more willing to help others do the same.

THE POWER OF AWE

Awe is the feeling of being in the presence of something vast that transcends our understanding of the world. In 1757, Irish philosopher Edmund Burke wrote in *A Philosophical Inquiry into the Origin of Our Ideas of the Sublime and Beautiful* that we feel awe not only during religious ritual or in communion with God, but also in everyday experiences—being moved by music, hearing thunder, watching a brilliant sunset, or being surrounded by towering trees. Awe is all around us.

Research suggests that we need meaning in life and work to function. The experience of awe has the potential to turn our lives in a new direction, giving us a new perspective on the world and our place in it. As Neil deGrasse Tyson put it: "I look up at the night sky and I know that we are part of this universe. We are in this universe. But perhaps more importantly than both of these facts is that the universe is in us." Studies show that being in awe of something greater than oneself promotes prosocial behavior and gives us a sense of purpose.

In 2015, a study by the University of California revealed that wonder has the power to make us more positive, more helpful, and friendlier. Subjects reported feeling less self-important; more humble; and more willing to help others, give to charity, or lessen their impact on the planet. They also reported feeling happier. Ongoing research into the power of awe is, if you'll pardon the expression, eye-opening.[24]

---

24 Paul K. Piff, et al., "Awe, the Small Self, and Prosocial Behavior," *Journal of Personality and Social Psychology* 108, no. 6 (2015): 883-899, http://dx.doi.org/10.1037/pspi0000018.

> Peak experiences are described by psychologist Abraham Maslow as "especially joyous and exciting moments in life, involving sudden feelings of intense happiness and well-being, wonder and awe, and possibly also involving an awareness of transcendental unity or knowledge of higher truth." If gazing up at a grove of tall trees surrounded by a nimbus of soft green light makes goosebumps ripple down your neck, you are experiencing awe.

Awe stops the clock. The experience of vastness slows our perception of time. Research by psychologists at Stanford University and the University of Minnesota shows that experiencing awe increases well-being, giving us the sense that we have more time available.[25] When experiencing awe, we are completely present, and time seems to stand still. We're off autopilot and 100 percent engaged with the experience. We're unlikely to be looking at our phones if we're taking in the majesty of the Grand Canyon for the first time.

Awe binds us to the collective. When we feel awe, we feel connected. Near Berkeley's Museum of Paleontology stands a grove of eucalyptus trees, the tallest in North America. A team of researchers had one set of participants look up into the trees for one minute, long enough for them to report feeling awe. A second set of participants were asked to look up at the façade of an impressive science building. Both groups then encountered a researcher pretending to stumble and drop a handful of pens on the ground. The participants who had been gazing up at the awe-inspiring trees picked up more

---

25 Melanie Rudd, Kathleen D. Vohs, and Jennifer Aaker, "Awe Expands People's Perception of Time, Alters Decision Making, and Enhances Well-Being," *Association for Psychological Science* 23, no. 10 (August 10, 2012): 1130-1136, https://doi.org/10.1177/0956797612438731.

pens than those who had not experienced awe. Awe binds us as individuals into a social identity and makes us kinder.

Awe tames the sabertooth. The negative emotions that drive our fight-flight-freeze response cause inflammation throughout the body as they increase cortisol and adrenaline production. Studies have shown that individuals who recall more experiences of awe in a month-long period have lower levels of cytokines (the proteins that cause all that inflammation) than those who did not harness awe. It turns out that beholding the night sky while camping near a river can be a powerful immune booster.

HARNESSING WONDER

Think of a time that you've experienced awe. How did that feel? It could be a spectacular hike, a vacation in a beautiful place, an inspiring story, or an incredible piece of music. There are, of course, experiences that are truly extraordinary (standing on the summit of Mount Everest or seeing the Grand Canyon for the first time) but there are also everyday experiences that are equally amazing and awe-inspiring.

I was watering my garden one summer when wonder dropped in for a visit. The watering process, done by hand, usually takes about two hours. I like to water early in the morning, enjoying a moment of quiet before the world wakes up. As I held the hose up to direct the stream of water, a tiny gleaming jewel caught my eye. Directly above the stream of water, almost touching my hand, a beautiful humming-bird hovered effortlessly, dipping its feet in the water in an astonishingly similar movement to humans paddling in a pool. Standing transfixed, I held my breath, not wanting to startle this little visitor. Every perfect feather etched in exquisite detail, it cocked its head and looked me squarely in the eye. We regarded each other for what felt like an eternity but must have been only moments. And then, just as quickly as it had appeared, the hummingbird was gone.

In a world that seems to move ever more quickly, this encounter left me with a sense of wonder. There is so much that is beautiful, and so much that we don't notice as we go about our hectic lives. So busy are we with email, texts, social media, and the double-edged sword of technology that keeps us constantly connected, we risk becoming disconnected from the spectacular world we live in. Recognition of those little, often mundane events in our lives gives us an opportunity to press the pause button, just for a moment, and experience the incredible beauty all around us.

Life is not measured by how many breaths you take, but by the moments that take your breath away. Awe is in the smile of a loved one, the kindness of people, the laughter shared with a colleague, the feel of a gentle breeze on your skin, the rise of the moon on a clear and starry night, or music that makes your heart soar. If we can harness wonder, we can start to see the world around us through a lens of positivity that builds optimism and reduces fear. Moments of wonder are all around us, every day. We only have to look up to see them.

MOMENTS OF WONDER ARE ALL AROUND US, EVERY DAY. WE ONLY HAVE TO LOOK UP TO SEE THEM.

THREE CALLS TO ACTION

1. Climb the wall. Looking at obstacles as opportunities to learn and grow makes it easier to overcome them.

2. Remember that pain is not permanent. Focusing our attention on resolution of a problem rather than rumination about the problem creates forward momentum.

3. Seek out the amazing. Taking the time to see the extraordinary in the everyday is key to cultivating an optimistic mind-set and increasing resilience.

CHALLENGE

PART II KEY TAKEAWAYS

Stephen Covey said: "Just as we develop our physical muscles through overcoming opposition, such as lifting weights, we must develop our character muscles by overcoming challenges and adversity." Looking for the opportunity in setbacks strengthens our ability to overcome them.

Dwight D. Eisenhower said: "The supreme quality for leadership is unquestionably integrity. Without it, no real success is possible, no matter whether it is on a football field, in an army, or in an office." Holding ourselves and others to a high ethical standard builds credibility, respect, and trust.

Thomas Huxley said: "Patience and tenacity are worth more than twice their weight of cleverness." In tough times, tenacity shows others that we're willing to stand up for what matters.

John F. Kennedy said: "As we express our gratitude, we must never forget that the highest appreciation is not to utter words, but to live by them." Appreciation is both a way to motivate others, and an elixir for life.

PART III

MOVE THROUGH FEAR
AND HARNESS MOTIVATION
TO FIND THE SILVER LINING

CHAPTER 7

FEEL THE FEAR, AND DO IT ANYWAY

When we let our light shine, we unconsciously give other people permission to do the same. As we are liberated from our own fear, our presence actually liberates others.
—*Marianne Williamson*

To be human is to know failure. It's an inevitable part of life. One of the frailties of the human psyche is our fear of failure. Yet without overcoming fear, we can't innovate, create, or push forward as we are paralyzed by it. Fear-based cultures are averse to innovation because of the possibility of failure. These cultures erode trust, destroy collaboration, and stifle creativity.

I had been on a small team for several years when the team was transferred into a larger group. On my first day in the new group, I walked into the building and immediately felt sick to my stomach. At first, I thought the problem was me. Perhaps I didn't know enough about the new organization—maybe I didn't fit in. Gradually it became clear that it wasn't only me. My co-workers were miserable and stressed, too. No one was having a good time, and the anxiety in the atmosphere was palpable. My physical reaction was not to the building, but to the fear-based energy of the group.

Management did not clarify expectations, instead changing the goals constantly and publicly ridiculing those who did not meet their shifting expectations. Managerial fear overpowered trust, eroding the confidence of even the most capable people. This caused the fear to spread, with a general lack of risk-taking and creativity leading to underperformance. In a confidence-sapping negative spiral, those who spoke up did so tentatively, which made them appear unsure. This created doubt in their capabilities, and management would interrogate them more aggressively. Their nervousness would increase, they became incapable of thinking clearly, and the situation deteriorated from there. A large portion of the workforce became disengaged, simply going through the motions each day. People were reluctant to take risks or act, even when the course of action was obvious. And if something went wrong, they were quick to find someone else to blame.

THE FOOTPRINT OF
A FEAR-BASED CULTURE

A workplace culture of permissiveness, blame, and inaction fosters bullying. Pervasive workplace bullying tends to start at the top, trickling down through the ranks, creating an entrenched cycle that is difficult to stop. If leaders normalize this behavior by indicating that it is acceptable—either by implicitly allowing others to join in the bullying or by failing to intervene—the trickle-down effect can be devastating.

A study in *Personnel Psychology* found that supervisors who perceive being excluded from decision-making (being ignored or denied the opportunity to offer input) often demonstrate abusive behavior toward their employees, generally in the form of angry outbursts. In the same vein, in research published in the *Academy of*

Management Journal, University of Minnesota psychologist Theresa Glomb, PhD, found that when a workplace establishes a bullying norm, other work-group members are more likely to act aggressively. Moreover, the people most likely to bully are those who feel bullied. "As such, one person's sense of being bullied can quickly engender a toxic workplace in which bullying spreads," she says. In fear-based cultures, leaders use aggression to gain control over their situation, and that manifests in bullying.[26]

A toxic culture is easy to spot, as telltale signs manifest:

- Autocratic leadership that refuses to include employees in key decisions.

- Stifled decision-making as power coalitions focus on serving their own interests.

- Fear of failure and being wrong as any setbacks are catastrophized and employees punished.

- Culture of blame and scapegoating as everyone strives not to become a target.

- Lack of risk-taking and a desire to remain invisible.

- Lack of two-way feedback mechanism between leadership and employees where leaders talk about collaboration, but no-one takes them seriously.

- Low-level griping and gossip about a common enemy rather than constructive dialog to resolve issues.

- Increase in employee sick days due to stress in the environment.

---

26   Theresa Glomb, "Interpersonal aggression in work groups: Social influence, reciprocal, and individual effects," *Academy of Management Journal* 46, no. 4 (January 1, 2003): 486-496, https://experts.umn.edu/en/publications/interpersonal-aggression-in-work-groups-social-influence-reciproc.

The underlying assumption of a fear-based culture is that stability and control are to be valued, largely at the expense of innovation, flexibility, and discretion. Fear doesn't bring out the best in people, but rather mutes their performance as they take fewer risks and make overly conservative, safe choices. The cost of complete safety is the complete loss of freedom.

Lack of trust becomes endemic, and after a certain point, the organization is at the mercy of the law of diminishing returns, as productivity is diminished and risk-taking is avoided at all costs. Employees who care deeply and want to make a difference find themselves at an impasse as they are unwilling to share great ideas. And in a place that repeatedly violates their values, they are mistreated by their friends and colleagues in a bizarre attempt to gain favor with management.

BREAKING OUT OF THE BOX

Schrödinger's cat is a thought experiment, sometimes described as a paradox, devised by Austrian physicist Erwin Schrödinger in 1935 to demonstrate quantum mechanics. In simple terms, Schrödinger stated that if you place a cat and something that could kill the cat (a radioactive atom) in a box and sealed it, you would not know if the cat was dead or alive until you opened the box, so that until the box was opened, the cat was (in a sense) both dead and alive. This is used to represent how scientific theory works. No one knows if any scientific theory is right or wrong until it can be tested and proved.

In the organizational context, a similar paradox can occur as we unwittingly seek comfort in familiar discomfort. Efforts to please their fear-inducing manager exhausted the employees in the team, and many of them broke down over time. As disengagement set in, they were less inclined to be creative or innovative. Instead, they did the bare minimum to survive while staying as invisible as possible. They were present physically, but out of necessity of self-preservation, and to protect themselves from the toxic environment, they became emotionally absent. Schrödinger's cat was imaginary, but the team's situation was very real, and a sad demonstration of being trapped in a situation in which they felt both alive—and dead.

Alan Briskin wrote in his book *The Stirring of Soul in the Workplace*: "The tragedy of individuals who have never known work to be anything but demeaning is that they begin to disintegrate physically, emotionally, and spiritually." I could certainly relate, and I left the team a few months later. The downstream effect of the toxic culture that had been created was a largely ineffective group that failed to deliver any benefit to the company. The team stagnated, and employees who tried to fight the culture disappeared without warning, as people spoke their names in whispers, if they mentioned them at all. Within a year, the entire group of more than two hundred people were laid off, and a function that had formerly been integral to the company's success simply ceased to exist. Many of the individuals who had suffered at the hands of the fear-based culture finally broke out of Schrödinger's box, joining new teams or other companies where they could shine.

CHALLENGING THE COMMITTEE

We all have experiences that color how we approach every aspect of our lives. Customers have past successes and failures that will influence their interaction with any product or service. Employees are no different. Each of them brings their own filter into every interaction. It is this filter that creates stories, myths, and legends to resolve confusion and provide direction for each of us as we search for meaning. Many times, these stories come from authority figures—

often family members, teachers, or others whose opinion means a great deal to us. And often, the stories are not kind.

When I finished high school, I had no idea what I wanted to be. I was eligible to go to college but had no specific passion to guide my decision around which field of study to pursue. I overheard my father say to my mother; "If she was anything special, it would have shown up by now." Words that would haunt me for years.

There is a saying that a committee is a life form with several mouths, but no brain. Each of us has an inner know-it-all in our heads telling us we're not good enough. We carry these voices with us throughout our lives, and they can hold us back when we need to move forward. Overcoming them means facing them head on and challenging the validity of the stories they are telling.

Early in my career in the United Kingdom, I was working as an executive assistant to the director of human resources and finance. Part of the director's role was to showcase the new infrastructure the company had put in place to track headcount, accounts payable, employee expenses, and invoicing. Back then, this system was revolutionary, having consolidated over two dozen disparate finance systems into a single streamlined experience. The director would walk customers through the system and then answer questions about implementation costs, system requirements, and so on.

On the day of a customer presentation that had been months in planning, barely an hour before the customer was due to arrive, the director called to let me know that he was ill and couldn't make the meeting. He asked me to find an alternate presenter, familiarize that person with the presentation, and introduce him or her to the customer. I asked every leader I could find in the office that day to help, but none of them were available to take the meeting. Given that the customer had flown in from Canada and was already in transit to our offices, canceling the presentation was not an option. I had no choice but to deliver the presentation myself. My father's words ran through my head. Who was I to think I could do this? Why would a customer possibly care about anything I had to say? The company would probably be insulted to have someone so low in the organizational hierarchy presenting to them.

With thirty minutes to spare and no surrogate in sight, I marshalled my resources. I had to create space for a new paradigm in my own mind and take action. I had helped the director create the presentation, and I had seen him deliver it multiple times. I knew it well. There was no reason I couldn't do this at least passably well. When the time came, I welcomed the customer and apologized for the change in plans. My palms were damp, and my voice shook as I launched into the presentation. Fortunately, the customer was very gracious, listening attentively and asking questions along the way. I'm convinced he intentionally didn't ask me any really tough questions, and for that, I was grateful.

When the director returned to the office, I fully expected him to be furious that I had assumed that I could step in for him. But when I sheepishly confessed what I had done, he was delighted and impressed. If I could do this, he told me, it was clear that I was capable of a great deal more. He promoted me into a communications role then and there, and my career got underway.

Challenging our committee is not easy. Our critical inner voice has the power to motivate or demean us. It is the product of side comments from other people that blend with our own views of ourselves, creating self-doubt. And it is ever-present. Focusing on understanding the way the voice helps or hinders us is key to moving past it.

Make peace with the past. When my father said I was nothing special, he meant that I had no special subject interest going into college. His words were not intended to be hurtful; he was simply making an observation about my interests, and yes, he phrased it poorly. While his words initially held me back, they have also galvanized me to take on challenges over the years. Making peace with the inner critic means looking at our stories without judgement.

Prove them wrong. When the voices in our heads start to get loud, we have a choice; we can let them overpower us, or we can challenge them. If the committee tells us we'll never achieve anything, we'll always be mediocre, or we're a fraud, we can consciously seek to validate whether these things are really true. Ask a trusted friend or colleague to help test the statements. Calling on past successes also serves as hard data that can help us challenge the negative assumption, move forward, and prove the committee wrong.

FINDING THE SILVER LINING
IN SPITE OF FEAR

I had been working in the United Kingdom for almost seven years when my manager asked me to act as mediator in a dispute between our recruiting team and a group of product managers who were implementing a new candidate-tracking system. The two factions were not getting along, and it was holding up the project. The product managers in the United States wanted to create a single candidate database that would eliminate spreadsheets on individuals' laptops and enable recruiters around the globe to access strong talent. The UK recruiting team, however, was quite comfortable with their spreadsheets and didn't particularly relish the idea of having their pool of candidates hijacked by other recruiters around the globe. We were at an impasse.

I knew nothing about recruiting or candidate-tracking systems and was vastly unqualified for the task. Nevertheless, I persevered, bringing the two parties together and helping them to look at the situation through the lens of a shared mission rather than divergent goals. As we focused on outcomes rather than positions, the UK recruiting team members slowly shifted their perspective, seeing the sharing of candidates as an opportunity to extend their own quality talent pool rather than as a threat. By establishing common ground—the desire to identify great candidates for the company—we were able to work together to launch the candidate-tracking system in record time.

A few months later, one of the United States team members called to tell me that she was leaving the group. Would I be willing to transfer to the United States and take on implementing the same candidate-tracking system around the world? The prospect of taking on a role I felt unprepared for, not to mention relocating to a new continent (again), was daunting. But Peter and I agreed that the opportunity was too good to pass up, and I said yes. Over the next two years, I partnered with the team to successfully launch the candidate-tracking system in eighty-two countries around the world, making plenty of mistakes along the way, but learning invaluable lessons from every one of them.

Fear is an inevitable emotion. We encounter it in all aspects of our lives, at work, at school, and at home. The key to success lies in how we manage fear. The leap of faith Peter and I took to come to the United States was more challenging than anything else I had experienced. But overcoming my fear also gave me opportunities to grow that I would otherwise not have had. For leaders, consistently overcoming fear is essential. Being tenacious in spite of fear takes courage of conviction and a strong belief in our choices. Leaders who are paralyzed by fear cannot fight for their causes and cannot fight for their teams. Fearless

FEARLESS LEADERS ARE NEVER TRULY WITHOUT FEAR.

leaders are never truly without fear; instead, they know how to find the silver lining in spite of it.

Be resolute. Motivation is not enough. Sheer willpower will not keep you motivated to stay the course. Effective leaders know that being motivated will get them started but won't get them through the rough days that lie ahead. Real dedication is the only thing that can empower this journey. And to find this, all leaders have to ask themselves just how resolute they really are. By understanding their level of commitment to the path and the reason for taking it, these leaders can tap into this internal resource when times get tough. Holding onto their "why" helps them power through fear.

Identify challenges. Visionary leaders anticipate setbacks. They are realistic about obstacles getting in the way of their goals, and they are ready to meet these challenges head-on. Some challenges are unavoidable; others are within our control. Leaders who recognize the difference put plans in place to overcome those that are in their control and minimize or accept those that are unavoidable. They assume there will be bumps in the road so as to be as prepared as possible to deal with them.

Practice positivity. A positive attitude buffers fear. Accomplished leaders know that a single negative event is not part of a never-ending pattern of defeat. If they mess up, they admit it, learn from it, and move on. Shifting our focus to a positive perspective breaks the paralyzing cycle of fearful rumination and galvanizes us back to action.

Detach from the outcome. Jack Canfield wrote: "If you want to remain calm and peaceful as you go through life you have to have high intention and low attachment." Effective leaders know that not always getting what they want or having things go their way is just a part of life. They are skilled at letting such things go, while maintaining forward momentum in the direction of the goal. By detaching from a particular outcome, leaders remain agile, embracing alternate possibilities and seeing opportunities that may otherwise have remained hidden.

We all deal with fear every day. The challenge is to feel that fear and move through it. We're all going to fall occasionally. Getting back on our feet is up to us. What a gift we give ourselves, our colleagues, our teams, and our communities if we can push through our fear and see the world of possibility that exists in every interaction, every relationship, and every experience of our lives.

THREE CALLS TO ACTION

1. Know what you stand for. A healthy culture takes constant dedication and focus and is well-reflected at the top by every executive in the organization.

2. Challenge the inner critic. Overcoming fear and moving forward in spite of it is not for the faint of heart. But the rewards for doing so are immeasurable.

3. Hope for the best but expect the worst. Anticipating setbacks, being prepared to address them, and learning from them when they do happen, builds a resilient mind-set that is focused on action.

CHAPTER 8

THE ROAD TO HIGH PERFORMANCE

Coming together is a beginning.
Keeping together is progress.
Working together is success.
—Henry Ford

Wouldn't it be great if we could just push a button and have motivated, energized, and engaged employees? Pressures in the business world grow as companies increasingly operate on a global scale, making motivation hard to come by. Customers need solutions quicker; investors need results sooner. Change is the new constant, and it comes with a healthy dose of fear. As we saw in the previous chapter, the ability to overcome that fear and adapt to change is crucial for survival. Leaders are faced with the challenge of inspiring their teams to keep moving forward in the face of challenges that may at times feel insurmountable. This means tapping into both the leader and the team's commitment to the mission, overcoming the fear that comes with the challenges they are facing, and working together to overcome them.

In 1965, psychologist Martin Seligman was doing research on classical conditioning, the process by which we associate one thing with another. In the Pavlovian tradition, Seligman would ring a bell and then give a light (harmless but painful) shock to a dog. After a few shocks, the dog started reacting to the shock before it happened. As soon as he heard the bell, the dog would react as though he had been shocked, regardless of whether he was in fact shocked or not.

Seligman took it a step further, putting several of the dogs into large crates that were divided by a low fence down the middle. The dogs could see the other side of the fence, and easily jump over it to the other side. One side of the crate was electrified; the other was not. When Seligman put the dogs on the electrified side of the fence and administered a light shock, he expected the dogs to jump to the non-electrified side of the crate. Instead, they lay down, not trying to escape the shocks at all. It seemed that the first part of the experiment had taught them that there was nothing they could do to avoid being shocked, so they simply gave up in the second part.

THE PAST HAD TAUGHT THEM THAT THEY WERE HELPLESS, AND DESPITE EVIDENCE TO THE CONTRARY, THEY HAD ACCEPTED THIS AS REALITY.

Seligman described their condition as learned helplessness. The past had taught them that they were helpless, and despite evidence to the contrary, they had accepted this as reality. Seligman repeated the second part of his experiment with dogs that had not been through the classical conditioning in part one. These dogs had not been previously exposed to shocks, and they all quickly jumped over the fence to escape the shocks when they were put into the crate.

What does this have to do with people? Research has shown that the way we view the negative events that happen to us can have an impact on whether or not we feel helpless. Whe... that we have no control over what happens to... think, feel, and act helpless. No one is born t... innate trait. It is a learned behavior, conditioned... in which we either truly have no control over... we believe that this is the case. Even when presented an option to avoid pain, we do not attempt to take it. The good news is that we can overcome this unhealthy way of thinking, replacing old beliefs with new and healthy beliefs and learning to have compassion for ourselves and others. No shocks required.

THE CURIOUS CASE OF CONTROL

Steven Covey said, "We are not a product of what has happened to us in our past. We have the power of choice." Research published in *The How of Happiness* by University of California psychology professor Sonja Lyubomirsky has shown that only 10

> 90 PERCENT OF OUR HAPPINESS IS BASED ON HOW WE PERCEIVE OUR CIRCUMSTANCES.

percent of our happiness is based on our actual circumstances. In other words, 90 percent of our happiness is based on how we perceive our circumstances. Perception is our reality. There are specific ways in which we can improve our happiness by shifting our perception and our locus of control.

Locus of control is a concept that psychologist Julian Rotter introduced in the 1950s to describe differing approaches to daily stressors. It refers to the notion that we each view life either as something we can control or something that controls us. People who believe that they have control over both their successes and failures have an *internal* locus of control. These individuals believe they can influence events and their outcomes. They tend to be happier and

ce less stress, and they are healthier and more satisfied with
in general.

In contrast, those with an *external* locus of control are more likely
to believe that their lives are driven by forces outside of their control.
For example, when receiving exam results, people with an internal
locus of control tend to praise or blame themselves and their abilities.
People with a strong external locus of control tend to praise or blame
external factors such as the teacher or the difficulty of the exam itself.
The latter individuals are more susceptible to depression and learned
helplessness. In his book *Learned Optimism: How to Change Your
Mind and Your Life*, Martin Seligman describes learned helplessness
as a principal characteristic of depression. Depressed people often
report a loss of self-esteem that is associated with learned helplessness. They may stop striving for goals and won't make the effort, even
when they're likely to succeed.

Locus of control is largely learned. Leaders with an external
locus of control can influence their people to attribute their successes
and failures to unknown causes. This pessimistic habit of thinking
can transform mere setbacks into disasters, exacerbating the cycle of
helplessness throughout the organization. Leaders with an internal
locus of control take responsibility for who they are, and for their
actions and performance. They believe that the buck stops with them
when it comes to the performance of their departments or organizations. They see others as having the ability to grow and will take
an active role in the development of their people. Their mind-set
enables their organizations to cope with uncertainty and adapt to
change more easily, and it acts both as a buffer against burnout and
a source of motivation.

MOTIVATING AND
DEMOTIVATING FORCES

The motivating effects of empowering leadership are well documented. The demotivating effects of relationship conflict are often underestimated. Studies show that empowering leadership and relationship conflict influences team members' motivation in opposite ways. Additionally, when relationship conflict is low, the positive influence of empowering leadership is amplified. Leaders who develop a cohesive and supportive team environment can mitigate the effects of conflict in the organization.

A culture of internal competition removes focus from competing in the marketplace to competing in the hallways, distracting employees as they protect fiefdoms and engage in turf wars at the expense of the business and their colleagues. Imagine two Marines running to take a hill and shooting each other so there would be no chance that the other would get more credit for doing so! Creative efforts are destroyed by competing executive agendas.

Leaders who recognize major constituencies, develop ties to their leadership, and manage conflict are often highly successful as they move up the corporate ladder. By negotiating compromises and building alliances in the best interests of succeeding together, effective leaders can break down the silos and fiefdoms that are created by internal competition. These leaders also enable employees to make suggestions around team structure, project focus, and resource allocation in an egalitarian manner. By engaging employees actively in decision-making, leaders benefit from a talented, free-spirited, motivated, and loyal workforce.

You have more power than you know. Ultimately, each of us is responsible for our own results. It's only human to have doubts and fears. Leaders who perceive failure as a setback or challenge—rather than as a personal reflection of their ability to succeed—encourage those who work for them to look at obstacles in the same way. It's a mind game, and those who can focus on the long-term goal in spite of challenges or obstacles are uniquely positioned to win.

You're not trapped. A crucial step toward overcoming learned helplessness is to recognize that it is not an inherent personality trait and that with perseverance it can it can be overcome. Realizing that not everything is within our control—and rather than using negative events as a reflection of inability, assessing those events to see if we could have performed better, prepared better or challenged ourselves more—helps to counteract the self-defeating mind-set that accompanies learned helplessness. There may be events that we were underprepared for or a skill we didn't acquire in time for "that job," however these setbacks in life can be viewed as challenges to be conquered, and opportunities to be embraced, rather than insurmountable and unchangeable forces.

THE MULTITASKING MYTH

Envision the always-on millennial, iPhone in one hand, switching effortlessly between emails and business reports on a laptop in the other. A vision of productivity in this wondrous age of digital technology, right?

Wrong. They are seriously dumbing themselves down.

Have you ever felt the triumph of control that comes with doing several things at once? Don't be fooled by that euphoric feeling—it's all a trick. Multitasking is a myth.

Think you're good at doing several tasks at the same time? Reading and listening to music? Doing email in meetings? Driving while talking on the phone (hands free of course)? Neuroscience research shows that the brain is physically incapable of multitasking.

Instead, we are switching tasks quickly—a start/stop process is going on in our brain. And as we switch, withdrawing our attention from one task to another, this creates a split-second in which the brain is in no-man's land. It's called a post-refractory pause. Think of it like a train switching

NEUROSCIENCE RESEARCH SHOWS THAT THE BRAIN IS PHYSICALLY INCAPABLE OF MULTITASKING.

tracks: as it leaves one track when the switch is thrown, for a second it is between tracks before lurching onto the other track. This start/stop/start process is rough on us; rather than saving time, it costs time (even very small micro seconds). It can feel as though we are losing control. It's also less efficient. Tasks become harder, and we make more mistakes. Multitasking is the science of screwing several things up at once. And over time it can be energy-sapping.

The origin of the word multitasking originated from the computer realm. The first use of the word is from 1966 in a magazine called Datamation. Multitasking is defined as use of a single CPU for the simultaneous processing of two or more tasks. Ironically, the CPU does not in fact multitask. Instead, it switches between tasks in a fraction of a second. Turns out it's no better at multitasking than the rest of us.

Tony Schwartz, president and CEO of The Energy Project, calls this a personal energy crisis. As the demands of technology increase, we expect our capacity to deal with it to increase. But the pace is unsustainable. The greater the performance demand, the greater the need to nurture recovery—to rest, reset, and recharge. "Human beings aren't designed to run like computers: at high speeds, continuously, for long periods of time. By mimicking them, they're ending up running us," he writes.[27]

The reality is we simply can't talk on the phone, read email, send an instant message, and watch YouTube videos all at the same time. Instead of cruising down the information superhighway, we're stepping on the gas and then hitting the brakes, over and over. The stop/start process reduces our IQ by as much as 10 points, causes mental blanks, and reduces our productivity by 40 percent, according to Dr. Julia Irwin, senior lecturer in psychology at Sydney, Australia's Macquarie University. Multitasking makes us stupid.

Don't believe me?

Take a small test that I ask the attendees in my high-performance workshops to try:

Draw two horizontal lines on a piece of paper. Now, have someone time you as you carry out the two tasks that follow:

On the first line, write: I am a great multitasker.

On the second line: write out the numbers 1-20 sequentially, like this: 1 2 3 4 5 6 7 8 9 10 11 12 13 14 15 16 17 18 19 20

How much time did it take to do the two tasks? Usually it's about twenty seconds.

Now, let's get multitasking.

Draw two more horizontal lines. This time, again having someone time you, write a letter on one line, and then a number on the line below, then the next letter in the sentence on the upper line, and then the next number in the sequence, changing from line to line.

So, you write the letter "I" on the top line, and then the number

---

27 Tony Schwartz, "We're in a New Energy Crisis. This One is Personal," *Harvard Business Review*, March 22, 2011, https://www.fastcompany.com/1742084/were-new-energy-crisis-one-personal.

"1" on the bottom line. Then switch back to the top line and write the letter "a" and then the number "2" on the bottom line and so on, until you complete both lines.

I am…

1 2 3…

How did it go that time? On average, my workshop attendees' time is double or more what it was on the first round. You possibly also made some errors, and you were probably frustrated since you had to "rethink" what the next letter would be, and then the next number. This same exercise works on something as simple as reciting the alphabet and counting from 1 to 26. It doesn't matter how simple the task is, or how much muscle memory we have in performing it.

Switch-tasking on something very simple or something often more complex at the same time makes any task more difficult, it takes longer, and it confounds our brains.

A summary of research examining multitasking on the American Psychological Association's website describes how so-called multi-tasking is neither effective nor efficient. The findings demonstrate that when we shift focus from one task to another, that transition is neither fast nor smooth. Instead, there is a lag time during which our brain must wrench itself from the initial task and then grab onto the new task. Remember the train switching tracks? This shift takes time (up to 40 percent more time than single/mono-tasking). The results are consistent for children doing their homework while watching TV to employees who show greater productivity when they don't check their email frequently.

Convinced that it's time to stop multitasking? Next time you're tempted, I invite you to give yourself the gift of single-tasking for a limited time instead, perhaps fifteen minutes, and see if you can complete the task better and faster with energy left to spare.

CHOOSE YOUR DISTRACTIONS

We all deal with distractions. In an increasingly connected world, it's difficult to put down the device and focus on only one conversation, one interaction, or one task. Looking around in any place where people have gathered, most of them will be looking at their phones, despite being with other people. Could we have lost the ability to communicate through any means other than through the screen on our device?

The reality is that if we're staring at a screen, we're not present. Our attention is split between the people we're supposed to be spending time with and that tweet or Facebook post that just can't wait. Being truly present is about mindfulness. As Thich Nhat Hanh said, "With mindfulness, you can establish yourself in the present in order to touch the wonders of life that are available in that moment." If we're not paying attention, we may miss what really matters.

> **WITH MINDFULNESS, YOU CAN ESTABLISH YOURSELF IN THE PRESENT IN ORDER TO TOUCH THE WONDERS OF LIFE THAT ARE AVAILABLE IN THAT MOMENT.**

If we subscribe to the single-tasking approach, then we must choose our distractions carefully. Distractions come in all shapes and sizes, and often without warning. Some of the usual culprits that distract us no matter what time of day it is are email and social media. Of course, that inbox isn't going to clear itself out, so we have to consciously decide when to tackle it. Instead of reacting to emails as they come into our inbox, turning off the email notification alert and scheduling a few times during the day when we are not at our most productive or energetic is a perfect time for this kind of work. Checking in on social-media feeds once in a while as opposed to throughout the day will also free up significant periods of time that can be used more productively.

Time of day also has an impact on our productivity. Some of us are more productive first thing in the morning, whereas others may like to ease into high-energy tasks later in the day. Creating a routine and following it consistently creates physiological energy spikes that can fuel us to power through a task. The repetition of the routine focuses the mind and trains our brains to reproduce that focus and keep us operating at our peak. Peak times are different for each of us. The key is finding yours and using it to get to your flow state. As Somerset Maugham says, "I write only when inspiration strikes. Fortunately, it strikes every morning at nine o'clock sharp."

If we are immersed in a task that demands a great deal of cognitive energy, it can take up to fifteen minutes to get back to the same level of immersion in that task after being distracted. When we are in a state where our work is flowing seamlessly, and we feel both challenged and capable, we're far more likely to deliver an outstanding result. According to Mihaly Csikszentmihalyi in his book *Flow*, flow is "the optimal state of consciousness where we feel our best and perform our best." The passage of time is unnoticed as we are completely immersed and present in what we are doing. It is this state that enables the most progress on any task and delivers satisfaction for a job well done. But this only happens if we can resist the urge to check things like email, social media, text messages, etc.

> IF WE ARE IMMERSED IN A TASK THAT DEMANDS A GREAT DEAL OF COGNITIVE ENERGY, IT CAN TAKE UP TO FIFTEEN MINUTES TO GET BACK TO THE SAME LEVEL OF IMMERSION IN THAT TASK AFTER BEING DISTRACTED.

Of course, even with all this planning, interruptions are inevitable. My husband and I share a home office, and we like to share interesting information and run things by each other throughout the day when we are together. This means stopping the flow of whatever we're focused on, and then picking up the task again. Phone calls, webinars, and online seminars present similar distractions. This can be challenging, particularly if immersed in a task that takes a lot of cognitive processing (like writing a book, for example).

The same problem presents itself in open-plan office designs. Initially designed to enable productivity through increased collaboration, a study of forty thousand workers in more than three hundred companies revealed that open-plan offices can be a productivity killer. Contrary to popular belief, people are not more productive in open-plan offices, and an Exeter University study showed both a 15 percent reduction in productivity and a 32 percent drop in well-being. For those working on complex tasks, the distractions can be overwhelming. Time-consuming distractions average eighty-six minutes per day, resulting in unproductive, overly stressed employees who, not surprisingly, take more sick leave.[28] According to *The New Yorker*, companies with open-plan offices can expect employees to take 62 percent more sick days.[29]

While open-plan offices are not going away, there are some options that can help those of us who are in these distraction-rich environments to get back on track. The nature of working environments is of course subjective, and different approaches will work better for different individuals.

Get focused. Paying attention to one sight or sound in the environment isolates it from others. This focuses the mind, enabling us to become fully present. Looking at a light for a few moments or

28 Toby Dantzic, "The Secret Life of Buildings," *The Telegraph*, August 2011, https://www.telegraph.co.uk/culture/tvandradio/8674789/The-Secret-Life-of-Buildings-Channel-4-preview.html.

29 Maria Konnikova, "The Open-Office Trap," *The New Yorker*, January 7, 2014, https://www.newyorker.com/business/currency/the-open-office-trap.

listening to a specific sound (rain outside the window, the hum of an air conditioner, birds chirping) can help us to regain focus and mindfully go back to what we were working on.

Stick to a schedule. Scheduling specific time frames to get the important tasks done helps us make the most of the time we have available to us. Making the most of natural energy peaks and taking breaks when energy ebbs trains your brain to anticipate cognitive loads and gets you into *flow* quicker.

Break it down and get it done. Procrastination is the enemy of efficiency. Focusing on getting the hard stuff out of the way now gives us more time to focus on the things we enjoy later. Ranking tasks in order of importance lets us know which ones to prioritize. And breaking down large goals into small, manageable tasks can also help us make progress, as we can enjoy the satisfaction of crossing items off that never-ending to-do list.

Turn off notifications. Not only are those beeps and pings distracting to others around us, they can often elicit a Pavlovian response as we stop what we're doing to check the incoming email or social-media update that is heralded by the sound. Using the "do not disturb" feature and turning your phone over so that you cannot see the screen, or even better, putting it away in a drawer while focusing on a task, can minimize temptation.

THREE CALLS TO ACTION

1. Do what you can with what you have. Taking responsibility for our actions and accountability for the outcome puts us back in control.

2. Stay on track. Single tasking enables us to reap the benefits of getting things done quicker, more accurately, and with less energy.

3. Choose conscious focus. Choosing our distractions carefully and matching tasks to our energy levels can boost productivity.

CHAPTER 9

WHAT WE NEED TO FLOURISH

I suppose leadership at one time meant muscles,
but today it means getting along with people.
—*Mahatma Gandhi*

O rganizations that want to have competitive advantage in the coming years will be focused on the emotional, mental, spiritual, and physical needs of their people. Leaders who empower their teams to bring more of themselves to work every day know that this demands a new way of working—a cultural shift. Culture is about more than hierarchy, infrastructure, systems, and tools. It's the place where technology and people intersect. In successful organizations, the structural hierarchy is used to ensure clarity of roles, responsibilities, and decision-making, but not to wield power.

The dominant coalition, if made up of those who have the interests of the organization at heart, can be leveraged to make decisions for the right reasons. And this same coalition can use the cultural frame to ensure that the values of the organization are strengthened and perpetuated through symbols and traditions. A strong, symbolic representation of cultural values in the form of both visual reminders as well as consistent behaviors, embodied by leaders within the company, is key to ensuring that these values are passed on to each employee. And as rituals, ceremonies, milestone celebrations, and traditions in line with those values are embraced and perpetuated, bonds are strengthened, and organizational health is increased. Inspirational leaders who bring others along are rare; when these individuals are supported by a structural environment that helps rather than hinders performance and productivity, organizational success is almost assured.

One of my favorite teams was focused on intentionally creating a culture of belonging and shared purpose in an organization historically divided by silos. We wanted to move the company's most senior technical community from an ad hoc group based on title or role to a value-producing, connected network. Our efforts focused on five critical levers: (1) improving information flow and knowledge reuse, (2) developing an ability to sense and respond to key problems or opportunities, (3) driving planned and emergent innovation, (4) nurturing value-creating interactions through shared experiences, and (5) building trust through community-engagement efforts.

Our approach was simple. Break down the silos, get them in a room together, and get them talking about mutual success. Integration of diverse efforts to ensure harmonious coordination is a key aspect of successful structural design. It is also the aspect that is most fraught with the danger of sub-optimization, with each disparate group focusing on their own goals rather than the overall mission. To address this, we created both vertical and lateral coordination through networks that reached across teams, creating a safe environment for discussion, debate, and constructive dissent. We set ground rules with zero tolerance for passive-aggressive behavior, and we placed strong emphasis on peer review to ensure that the focus was on learning from and supporting each other, not competing with each other. Creating a group that shared responsibility for a meaningful whole instead of a piece of that whole helped them to see the benefits of working together, creating collective accountability for results, reducing fear, and building trust.

A CULTURAL (R)EVOLUTION

The values shared by individuals in an organization are its heart and soul. But the company's culture always starts with the leader. It starts with a belief that every one of their people can grow and develop; that potential is nurtured, not pre-determined; and that everyone can become a key contributor to the mission. Embracing a culture of capability empowers teams to grow and achieve greatness. The tricky part is keeping the culture alive and strong as the company grows. Leaders who wish to cultivate this kind of culture know that they cannot do this alone. Fostering a positive, productive, and resilient workplace culture takes a steady hand, firm resolve, and support at every level of the organization.

When General Stanley McChrystal took command of the Joint Special Operations Task Force in 2003, he knew that to succeed he needed to put a network in place that would combine transparent communication with decentralized decision-making authority. He broke down silos and leveraged best practices from small units that could be scaled around the globe. And he built teams that were interdependent on each other to get the job done. In his book, *Team of Teams*, McChrystal writes, "A fighting force with good individual training, a solid handbook, and a sound strategy can execute a plan efficiently, and as long as the environment remains fairly static, the odds of success are high. But a team fused by trust and purpose is much more potent. Such a group can improvise a coordinated response to dynamic, real-time environments." Whether taking on terrorists or running a business, leaders who trust and empower their teams to navigate a changing environment well are on the winning side.

Business is a contact sport. Leaders who want to build trust in a team know that the team has to trust them first. These leaders recognize the signs of mistrust and deal with them quickly. They set clear expectations for the team, focusing their energies on important issues to minimize organizational politics. The strongest teams are made up of individual members who don't want to let each other down and leaders who put individual accountability in place.

Expect personal accountability. A culture of resilience is one that embraces continual evolution. And that evolution happens from the ground up. While General McChrystal trusted his team to deliver, he also demanded "extreme participatory transparency." All participants in the business of taking down a terrorist organization had to be fully aware of their shared purpose. McChrystal had to be clear about the details of the plan the team was proposing; then he let them execute. This shared consciousness, coupled with strong lateral connectivity across teams, ensured cooperation across silos and the desire to work together to succeed.

Leaders who infuse a sense of personal leadership and accountability for delivering results at every level understand what motivates their employees and what drives them to succeed. Then they tap into that motivation to help them to do so. It takes a leader who is willing to embrace vulnerability by stepping back and letting the team take the lead.

VULNERABILITY IS NOT FOR THE FAINT OF HEART

Mother Teresa said, "Honesty and transparency make you vulnerable. Be honest and transparent anyway." Many leaders feel vulnerable asking for help or admitting that they were wrong. But doing so strengthens integrity. Mistakes are an inevitable part of leadership. As John Wooden said: "If you're not making mistakes, then you're not doing anything." Leaders who own their mistakes and learn from them gain respect. And when they ask for support, they create opportunities for others to share their talent and creativity and feel pride in helping. Doing so forges a deeper relationship and strengthens trust.

LEADERS WHO OWN THEIR MISTAKES AND LEARN FROM THEM GAIN RESPECT.

At Ford, CEO Lee Iacocca walked the floor regularly, asking for advice, creating a safe space for opinions from his employees at every level in the organization. He didn't make any assumptions about his ability to know what was going on day-to-day without asking the people who were actually doing the work. He listened to what they had to say before he made decisions.

Anders Knutsen, CEO at Bang & Olufsen, sat on the floor handing out wage checks, drank beer with shop stewards on the plane back from fights in labor court, and entered the canteen to meet with employees who threatened to strike (when the rest of management wouldn't). His ability to connect with employees at every level made him relatable and approachable, and his attitude of seeking to understand the needs of his teams helped resolve what appeared to be irreconcilable issues.

Both leaders were willing to be vulnerable, and to admit that they didn't have all the answers. In doing so, they opened themselves up to different perspectives, harnessed the wisdom of their teams, and found solutions that they otherwise may have missed.

Separate people from the problem. Focusing on an issue to be resolved rather than the personalities behind it helps us find win-win solutions without devolving into personal attacks. This approach also insulates us from becoming victims of attack on a personal level. Organizational effectiveness is largely dependent on a leader's political skill, and in some instances, a collaborative strategy may be less effective than a more adversarial approach. But focusing on sharing information, building relationships, and formulating an agenda aligned with our values and ethical principles will always be a more constructive approach to building and leveraging power than wielding it like a club.

Be willing to change. For many of us, failing at something that is important to us, a job or relationship for example, may impact our self-esteem, because our self-worth is tied to them. Not so for those with humility. Leaders who have a sense of the intrinsic value of being human at work can withstand failure or criticism. They have an accurate picture of themselves—both their faults and their gifts—which helps them navigate change by seeing what they need to change within, without distortion. When they inevitably fail at something, it doesn't mean that they are failures. It just means they're human.

Great leaders know that to impact their communities and organizations, they have to change themselves. The paradox is that this change takes humility, something that leaders can see as a sign of weakness, but that in reality takes great courage.

DARE TO BE HUMBLE

In a society that is increasingly narcissistic and seemingly more focused on climbing the corporate ladder or the number of friends on Facebook, humility seems hard to come by. Our culture places enormous value on self-aggrandizement and external accomplishment, often to the detriment of modesty. Leaders often fall into the trap of mistaking arrogance for authority, particularly when competence and credibility are important to them.

I had the privilege of having a friend who was a powerful example of humility. An ex-NASA engineer who trained astronauts to survive the ravages of space, he was extremely well read, with an off-the-charts IQ. A gifted photographer, he shared his love of the world around him by capturing the beauty of it with infinite patience. These gifts he kept in humble perspective, never making another person feel less significant. Painfully honest about his faults, and eager to learn from the example of others, he was insatiably curious, and there were very few topics of which he didn't have extensive knowledge. Despite this, he was always open to opinions from others, often saying that the more he learned, the less he knew. When he passed away, hundreds attended his memorial service to celebrate the life of a truly incredible human being.

Cultivate compassion. Humble leaders are the ones who can accept their own limitations without defensiveness, cultivate compassion for the limitations of their employees, and set aside their egos for the good of the organization. They recognize that none of us are perfect and believe that others have the capability to work on their limitations by being open to new perspectives, ideas, and advice. Their willingness to be vulnerable, confess their errors, and retrace their steps to correct them (often with the help of others) cultivates inner strength and builds resilience. They are less likely to act aggressively or manipulate or blame others for failures. By taking responsibility for their mistakes and listening to others' ideas, they can correct errors without negatively impacting their self-esteem.

Guide without ego. Leaders who are humble know that the main reason for emotional disengagement is when their employees are made to feel lost, embarrassed, or "slow." Helping employees to see the path ahead and to overcome their doubts and fears requires a leader with confidence. Preparing teams for the challenges they are going to face along the way requires a leader with tenacity and patience. Removing roadblocks and empowering people to succeed requires a leader with a clear vision and an ability to articulate that vision. These leaders are not arrogant; they are willing to set aside their ego to guide, support, and lead their employees with humility rather than arrogance. They lead from the heart. And this makes them leaders others want to follow.

THREE CALLS TO ACTION

1. Find the balance. Understanding patterns of dependence and interdependence enables strategic leaders to leverage influencers and coalitions effectively to gain support for complex and long-range decisions.

2. Embrace the inevitability of change. By anticipating obstacles and being prepared for them, we can focus where we are going and what we are setting out to accomplish, moving around change effectively to get there.

3. Lead with humility. Having the courage to admit we can benefit from the expertise of others with less power than us creates teams that share autonomy and mutual responsibility for success.

CONTROL

PART III KEY TAKEAWAYS

Ernest Hemingway said: "The best way to find out if you can trust somebody is to trust them." Leaders who encourage teams to share their opinions without fear of judgment or retribution create a highly motivated and productive workforce that freely shares information and collaborates in a climate of trust.

Abraham Lincoln said: "Nearly all men can stand adversity, but if you want to test a man's character, give him power." Power isn't about control, it is about strength. A leader is someone willing to give that strength to others so that they can stand on their own.

John Maxwell said: "A good leader is a person who takes a little more than his share of the blame and a little less than his share of the credit." Creating a culture of personal accountability means demonstrating a high level of ownership to achieve organizational results while trusting others to share the same level of responsibility.

Ralph Waldo Emerson said: "A great man is always willing to be little." Humble leaders actively seek the ideas and unique contributions of the employees they serve, creating a culture of learning and an atmosphere that encourages others to become the very best they can.

PART IV

COMMIT TO THE JOURNEY BY RENEWING RESOURCES TO NURTURE RECOVERY

CHAPTER 10

NURTURING RECOVERY

The only resources that last are those that we renew.
—Tony Schwartz

We all deal with constant digital demands, long hours, and time away from our families as we juggle hectic travel and work schedules. As a result, too often we're not working at full capacity. So often we are so busy learning to filter our reactions to stress that we forget that to navigate the day-to-day effectively and build resilience, we have to take care of ourselves. There is a reason that air stewards tell us to put our own oxygen masks on first in an emergency. If we're passed out on the floor of the plane, we're in no position to help others.

For leaders, nurturing recovery is critical to dealing with the demands of the digital age. Being able to recover from the inevitable ups and downs that we all encounter is crucial to our well-being. Taking care of ourselves also serves as an

FOR LEADERS, NURTURING RECOVERY IS CRITICAL TO DEALING WITH THE DEMANDS OF THE DIGITAL AGE.

example to those around us and ensures that we're able to contribute at the highest level.

A colleague who works with horses uses the term "step and rock back" to help clients understand at a physiological level when they need to demonstrate a calm demeanor when handling horses. Horses respond to emotional honesty and whole body communication, and people are no different. By taking a step backward, our energy becomes calm and renewing, allowing us to refocus and move forward again with purpose.

Here are some ways to step and rock back to nurture our recovery from stress.

BREATHE RIGHT

Not all breaths are created equal. Most of us breathe shallowly the majority of the time. And it's worse when we're stressed or anxious. The vagus nerve, which originates in the brain stem and extends all the way down to the tongue, vocal chords, heart, lungs, and other internal organs, is an important element of the parasympathetic nervous system (the system that controls our rest, relaxation, and digestion response and calms us down). When stimulated, the vagus nerve will counteract the sympathetic nervous system (the system responsible for activating our fight-flight-freeze response and causing us stress). When the vagal response kicks in, it reduces our heart rate and blood pressure, releasing an array of anti-stress enzymes and hormones such as prolactin, vasopressin, acetylcholine, and oxytocin. It tames inflammation, allergic responses, and tension headaches, relieving anxiety and depression.

To calm your nervous system and stimulate the vagus nerve, try some belly breathing. Diaphragmatic breathing is characterized by an expansion of the abdomen instead of the chest. Take a deep inhalation through your nose while counting to five, hold your breath for a count of six, and then slowly exhale while counting to seven.[30] Studies show that about ten minutes of deep breathing is sufficient to calm us down. The key is to have the breaths come from your belly, and slow down the exhale as much as possible.[31]

A client was experiencing a great deal of stress at work, and his health started to suffer as a result. He wasn't sleeping well, and he was increasingly short-tempered. After long days in the office, he was unable to stop worrying about work enough to enjoy quality time with his family. He took to locking himself away in front of the television for several hours every evening when he came home, trying to clear his head and relax. Clearly, this wasn't a sustainable solution.

We agreed that deep breathing during his commute home in the evenings might help to calm his active mind, letting him disengage from work to re-engage with his family. It didn't happen right away, but after a few weeks of consistent deep breathing, he reported feeling more relaxed when he got home. He was able to set aside the work day and be fully present with his family when he walked in the door. While not a panacea, breathing right helped him stop the endless cycle of work-day rumination, allowing him to focus on what mattered most.

SLEEP LIKE A CAVEMAN

Sleep is more than beauty rest. It's also brain rest and is one of the most important aspects of well-being. A good night's sleep keeps our

---

30 S. Z. Wang, S. Li, et al., "Effect of slow abdominal breathing combined with biofeedback on blood pressure and heart rate variability in prehypertension," *J Altern Complement Med* 16, no. 10, (October 2010): 1039-45, doi: 10.1089/acm.2009.0577.

31 Jon Kabat-Zinn, *Full Catastrophe Living (Revised Edition): Using the Wisdom of Your Body and Mind to Face Stress, Pain, and Illness* (New York: Bantam, 2013).

heart healthy, reduces stress, makes us more alert, reduces chronic inflammation, improves our memory, can help us lose weight, and may even prevent cancer.

Our minds are surprisingly busy while we're snoozing. In a process called consolidation, we strengthen memories or practice skills we learned while awake. If we're trying to learn something, we perform better after we sleep. In addition to consolidating memories, our brain reorganizes and restructures them, which can make us more creative. Researchers at Harvard University and Boston College found that we strengthen the emotional components of a memory during sleep, which may help spur the creative process. Ever slept on a problem only to come up with the perfect solution the next day?

A mouse study by the National Institute of Health suggests that sleep helps restore the brain by flushing out toxins that build up during waking hours, reducing the risk of Alzheimer's.[32] One of the waste products removed from the brain during sleep is beta amyloid, the substance that forms sticky plaques associated with the disease. As we sleep, the flow of cerebrospinal fluid in the brain increases, washing away the toxic waste proteins that build up between brain cells during the day. Our brain needs this sleep cleaning cycle. It is not possible for it to clean itself and keep us sharp and functioning well during the hours that we're awake. Without the cleaning cycle, we feel groggy and struggle to think clearly after a sleepless night. It takes at least three ninety-minute sleep cycles to get the benefits of memory consolidation that comes with NREM sleep.

Sleep affects our quality of life. Inflammation is linked to heart disease, stroke, diabetes, arthritis, and premature aging. Research

---

32   "How Sleep Clears the Brain," National Institutes of Health, October 28, 2013, https://www.nih.gov/news-events/nih-research-matters/how-sleep-clears-brain.

indicates that people who get six or fewer hours of sleep a night have higher blood levels of inflammatory proteins than those who get six hours or more. Studies have shown that C-reactive protein, which is associated with heart-attack risk, is higher in people who get six or fewer hours of sleep a night. British researchers discovered that fewer than five hours of sleep doubles the risk of death from cardiovascular disease—the number-one cause of death in the United States.

Lack of sleep also impacts performance. In US Army studies of marksmen, accuracy was measured based on how much sleep they got the night before. The results were astonishing. Those who had at least seven hours were 95 percent accurate, while those with only five hours of sleep were only 70 percent accurate. At four hours they were down to 50 percent accuracy, and three hours or less resulted in 15 percent accuracy. Health for the Army means that their soldiers are fit, ready, and resilient.[33] An adequate duration and continuity of sleep is critical to sustain performance. As General George Patton might have put it: "The idea is not to give up sleep for your country but to make the other poor bastard give up sleep for his."

A few things make your environment more conducive to sleep:

Clear the clutter. Eliminate books, magazines, empty water glasses, and other clutter from nightstands. Mess sends wakefulness-oriented alerts to our brains—it screams "look at me, read me, check your email!" To give your brain a rest, make your bedroom an oasis of calm and relaxation.

Go to the dark side. Our ancestors used to sleep in caves without artificial light, and our bodies still rely on the complete absence of

---

33 Marriott BM, ed., *Food Components to Enhance Performance: An Evaluation of Potential Performance-Enhancing Food Components for Operational Rations* (Washington, DC: National Academies Press, 1994).

light to cue us to sleep. Getting blackout blinds and losing the night light can help. If you have an alarm clock, turn the illuminated face away from you as even that small amount of light can trigger you to lie awake. Technology's favorite color also isn't doing us any favors. Blue light from screens and LED lights affect our sleep rhythms by inhibiting the production of melatonin, our sleep hormone. Our brain thinks the glow from the phone is the morning sun, so it's harder to stay asleep.

Harvard researchers found that 6.5 hours exposure to blue light suppresses melatonin twice as long (3.5 hours versus 1.5 hours) than exposure to green light. The University of Toledo found that blue light causes vital molecules in our eyes to become toxic, killing photoreceptor cells in the retina that do not regenerate. Blue light leaves visual artifacts (the after image of something bright that appears in a darkened room). UV- and blue-light-filtering eyewear can help, and blue-light filters are available for phones and PCs. Most importantly, banish blue light from your bedroom. That means no phone, backlit device, or television for at least an hour before bedtime. Let's not panic. We can do this.

Stay cool. Experts suggest that we sleep best in a room between sixty-five and seventy degrees Fahrenheit with adequate ventilation. Any colder and we may struggle to fall asleep. When we go to sleep, our set point for body temperature goes down. In a room that is too cold, the body struggles to achieve this set point. If the room is too hot, we're more likely to wake up in a tangle of bedsheets. The comfort level of our bedroom temperature also affects the quality of REM sleep, the stage in which we dream. Find the sweet spot that works for you.

Stick to a schedule. Turning in and getting up around the same time every day sets our internal sleep/wake clock. Erratic sleep patterns leave us feeling groggy and irritable, as brains love routine and our circadian rhythm needs a regular schedule to operate at its best. Changing a sleep schedule overnight is not possible, however. Making small changes slowly, in fifteen-minute increments over several days can help you adjust your sleep schedule. By picking a bedtime and wake-up time and sticking to them as much as possible, we enable our body's internal clock to get accustomed to the schedule. Insufficient sleep also decreases levels of the satiety-signaling hormone leptin and increases levels of the hunger-instigating hormone ghrelin. We lose our hunger control and eat more. Ideally, try to be in bed by ten o'clock in the evening. Any later, and you could consume up to 549 more calories per day.[34]

DO (NEARLY) NOTHING

We all struggle with the notion of wasted time. We think that unless we are busy getting things done, we are somehow slacking. But taking the time to do (nearly) nothing occasionally opens our minds to creativity, innovation, and possibilities we may not otherwise have seen.

Make a morning ritual. Instead of wrestling with your phone the minute you open your eyes, be gentle with yourself, waking up a little earlier, stretching, taking a long shower, or listening to music. Whatever feels inspirational and relaxing is a great way to start the day.

1. Take some deep breaths to activate the parasympathetic nervous system and counteract the high levels of cortisol that we experience in the morning.

2. Have one thought of gratitude to focus on the good and build optimistic neural pathways.

---

34 Rickey E. Carter and James A. Levine, "Lack of Sleep May Increase Calorie Consumption," National Sleep Foundation, accessed January 3, 2019, https://www.sleepfoundation.org/sleep-news/lack-sleep-may-increase-calorie-consumption.

3. Set a positive intention for the day by contemplating how you would like to feel looking back on today.

Go outside. Nature is a powerful tool for rebalancing the body and mind. It enables us to tap into our natural sense of wonder and has even been proven to lower heart rate and blood pressure, reduce stress-hormone production, boost immune system, and improve overall feelings of well-being. Nippon Medical School in Tokyo measured the activity of human natural killer cells in the immune systems of people before and after a visit to the woods. They saw significant increases in the cell activity immediately, and for up to a month following a weekend in the woods.

The practice of forest bathing has become wildly popular in recent years. Scientists have discovered that various essential oils, generally called phytoncide, are emitted by trees to protect themselves from germs and insects. Forest air doesn't just feel fresher and better—inhaling phytoncide seems to actually improve immune-system function. A thirty-minute walk in a green space improves our mood and self-esteem, reduces hostility and depression, and can even help attention disorders.[35]

Waste time well. Taking time each day to step away from the day-to-day regenerates us and increases energy. By giving ourselves white-space time, where we have no agenda, no deadline and nothing specific to get done, we create space to give ourselves whatever we need. The point is not to decide what that is until you begin. Sitting in a cozy chair away from work or household projects for a few minutes several times a day, stretching, or taking a walk lets us notice

---

35 Jeffrey Craig and Susan L. Prescott, "Here's Why a Walk in The Woods or a Dip in The Ocean Is So Great For Your Health," Science Alert, February 2016, http://www.sciencealert.com/here-s-why-a-walk-in-the-woods-or-a-dip-in-the-ocean-is-so-great-for-your-health.

the serenity in the moment and helps us reenergize and refocus. If thoughts come up, let them pass, and return your focus to something tranquil in your line of sight. This form of meditation is easy to do and can be done anywhere. As Ferris Bueller said: "Life is short. If you don't stop and look around once in a while, you might miss it."

> **LIFE IS SHORT. IF YOU DON'T STOP AND LOOK AROUND ONCE IN A WHILE, YOU MIGHT MISS IT.**

ENERGIZE YOUR BODY

The typical US adult is sedentary for 60 percent of his or her waking hours and sits an average of six to eight hours per day.[36] Too much sitting decreases the activity of an enzyme called lipoprotein lipase (LPL), which burns fat. As a result, we are at greater risk of becoming obese. Sitting for extended periods also decreases bone-mineral density without increasing bone formation, increasing the risk of fracture. It increases blood pressure and decreases the diameter of our arteries—all of which lead to increased risk of heart disease.

Studies in the US, Canada, Australia, and Asia have found an association between being sedentary and the risk of early death. If we sit more than six hours per day, we are at 40 percent greater risk of death over the next fifteen years. And here's the worst part—it doesn't matter how much we exercise. Sitting is the new smoking.

> **SITTING IS THE NEW SMOKING.**

Get on your feet. Replacing two hours of sitting with two hours of standing every day lowers blood sugar and cholesterol (and

---

36 Myanna Duncan, Aadil Kazi, and Cheryl Haslam, "Office workers spend too much time at their desks, experts say," British Psychological Society, January 15, 2012, https://www.sciencedaily.com/releases/2012/01/120113210203.htm.

burns calories!). Research shows that walking also enhances creative thinking, so walking while on the phone or when brainstorming can help us generate ideas. Working at a standing desk or taking a two-minute walk every hour can help offset the negative health effects from prolonged sitting. Combined with regular exercise in the form of strength training and cardio several times per week, getting on your feet can decrease your risk of heart disease, diabetes, and premature death.

Watch your posture. Posture and health are closely related, as posture affects every physiologic function, from breathing to blood pressure. Posture and motion don't only affect how long we live, but also how well we live. People with strong posture recover faster from injuries, exercise more effectively, have less pain, and even look more youthful. Posture even affects our mood, with good posture generating a more positive outlook. Whether we're standing or sitting, paying attention to our spine and keeping our back straight is good for both body and mind. Channel your mother telling you to stop slouching, and you'll feel better for it.

Appreciate your feet. All day long our feet carry us without complaint. (OK, maybe they complain a little.) To relieve stress, rolling a tennis ball along the length of your soles for a few minutes before bedtime, or getting a reflexology massage may stimulate the flow of vital energy to the brain. Foot massage can promote a state of deep relaxation, improving the quality of our sleep, relieving headaches (including migraines), and even reducing anxiety and depression.

EAT, DRINK, AND BE HEALTHY

Leanne started experiencing severe mood swings that were affecting her work. She would be happy one minute and sad the next. She was easily irritated, and it wouldn't take much to set her off. This was out of character for her, as she was a naturally happy, outgoing, and friendly person. Frustrated by her inability to control how she was feeling, she sought medical help. Her doctor quickly diagnosed her with bipolar disorder and recommended treatment with Lithium, a maintenance treatment for the disorder that comes with a host of potential side effects. Having recently qualified as a pilot, Leanne was reluctant to embark upon a medication regimen that would disqualify her from flying. She sought a second opinion from a naturopath, who recommended that she start taking large doses of high-quality fish oil to increase her omega-3 levels. The results were almost instantaneous. Her moods leveled out, and she has been happily flying ever since.

Amp up the healthy fats. Omega-3s help increase the levels of dopamine, a neurotransmitter associated with our reward response, and serotonin, a neurotransmitter associated with our ability to access feelings of well-being. The typical Western diet has an over-abundance of omega-6 (found in typical vegetable oils), which has been linked to inflammation on the brain associated with depression.

The power of omega-3s—helping to protect our cardiovascular systems, normalizing and regulating triglyceride levels in the blood, reducing LDL cholesterol (the bad kind) and elevating HDL levels (the good kind)—cannot be overstated. They discourage and reduce inflammation in the body, and play a preventive role against diseases like lupus, rheumatoid arthritis, and even cancer. They support healthy brain-cell structure and contribute to the overall flexibility and fluidity of brain-cell membranes. And—as if that weren't enough—they regulate the flow of proteins and neurotransmitters, which act as chemical messengers and are associated with fluctuations in mood.

Eating two or more servings of seafood like wild salmon, mackerel, or sardines per week will increase omega-3 fatty acids in your diet. For those who prefer not to eat fish—seaweed, leafy greens, avocados, cauliflower, and brussels sprouts are abundant in omega-3s. Throw in some omega-3 powerhouses like walnuts and brazil nuts, and you'll keep your brain in good shape.

Start the day with produce. Fruit is anywhere from 60–95 percent water in composition, depending on which fruit we choose. This means we're rehydrating after a night of dehydration. Starting off the day with fruit can help us avoid the mid-morning slump because they are easy to digest and can help flush toxins from our systems. Having the first meal of the day be produce eases our digestion into gear rather than overloading it first thing. Fruit also fills the energy tank with glucose, the vital fuel every cell in our bodies needs to function, along with antioxidants that prevent cellular damage and fiber that helps cleanse the digestive tract. Smoothies are a great way to benefit from all the fiber that the fruit and vegetables have to offer.

Hydrate all day. We lose fluids continuously, from skin evaporation, breathing, and waste elimination. Our cellular membranes are hydrophilic (water-loving), so it stands to reason that hydration is crucial for us to function. Water makes up 60 percent of our bodily fluids responsible for functions like digestion, circulation, transportation of nutrients, and regulation of body temperature. Unfortunately, when we don't drink enough water, our body can send mixed signals on hunger. Dehydration causes us to believe we need to eat when we really need to take in liquid. Cue the repeated visits to the refrigerator for snacks. Drinking water or unsweetened herbal tea consistently throughout the day can help us avoid mindless snacking due to thirst. Drinking a glass of water and waiting ten minutes is a good test of whether you're feeling hunger or thirst. If the thought of a piece of broccoli makes your mouth water just as much as a piece of chocolate, you're probably hungry.

Put down the fork. Mindless eating happens when we're bored, stressed, or anxious. It also happens when we're distracted. More times than I can count I have looked down to see only the remnants of crumbs to show for the sandwich I ate at my desk, with no memory of doing so. By turning off the TV, stepping away from the laptop, and putting down the phone, we can focus our senses on experiencing the texture, flavor, temperature, taste, and scent of our food. And the benefits don't stop at enjoying our meal. We also start to notice when we reach satiety (when our brain signals: that's enough nutrients, put down the fork) rather than mindlessly eating the entire bag of potato chips in one sitting and reaching satiation (when our stomach signals: that's way too much food, we're stuffed, stop eating). The catch is we only pick up these signals if we're paying attention.

THREE CALLS TO ACTION

1. Make every breath count. Consistent, focused attention on our breathing provides immediate and long-term benefits, reducing blood pressure and reducing the stress response.

2. Throw out the badge of honor. Lack of sleep is nothing to be proud of. Each hour of sleep missed means a 37 percent increase in risk of high blood pressure. Get in touch with your circadian rhythms.

3. Get moving to manage stress. Exercise reduces levels of stress hormones and stimulates the production of endorphins and distracts us from daily worries. Meditation in motion helps you remain calm and clear in everything you do.

COMMIT

PART IV KEY TAKEAWAYS

Byron Pulsifer said: "Breathing is more than just lungs inhaling and expelling. It is more about using life to its fullest." Every breath we take is an opportunity to make different choices and live life well. Use it wisely.

The Dalai Lama said: "Sleep is the best meditation." Regular, consistent sleep patterns help us repair our bodies and minds, making sleep the ultimate stress-management tool.

Virginia Woolf wrote: "One cannot think well, love well, sleep well, if one has not dined well." The nature of the foods we eat affects our emotional and mental well-being. To affect your mood, pay attention to your food.

Wilhelm von Humboldt said: "True enjoyment comes from activity of the mind and exercise of the body; the two are ever united." Exercise is the most underutilized antidepressant. Our bodies have evolved to move. Move well to feel well.

CONCLUSION

STEPPING OVER THE LINE

Life isn't about waiting for the storm to pass.
It's about learning to dance in the rain.
—*Vivian Greene*

Peter often tells me stories about his days in junior school. Like adolescent boys the world over, the way to sort out differences back then was to meet behind the woodworking shed after school and duke it out. As the two contenders took the measure of each other, a crowd would gather around them in a tight circle, and a line would be drawn in the sand between the opponents. Until one of them stepped over the line, no punches were thrown. Stepping over the line was the signal to commence battle.

The sabertooth is not going anywhere soon, and it will continue to evolve as our world becomes faster paced and more demanding. To take on the sabertooth, we must be willing to step over the line.

A LOOK BACK AT THE FOUR CS
OF RESILIENCE

Communicate with clarity, humility, and authenticity to inspire others to follow

Leaders have the power to inspire others through communication that creates clarity and generates energy. For many leaders, this becomes more challenging as their business grows, and as they move farther away from the day-to-day work. Some feel unsafe and vulnerable admitting that they're wrong, asking for help, or sharing the concerns they have as a leader. The resistance to doing so often stems from fear of failure, rejection, and humiliation. We want to feel powerful, rather than vulnerable. But humility and emotional courage is critical to being an effective communicator and a powerful leader.

Communication is a key element of making others feel that they are part of a bigger whole, with a sense of belonging and shared purpose. This takes clarity of vision and the ability to break it down into a manageable plan that can be communicated to others. It also takes creating a personal connection to enable employees to feel engaged and valued. That personal connection enables leaders to bring others along as they craft the vision. Teams who feel they have a real voice are those who become strong advocates for the vision.

Espousing the company values is not enough. Leaders who demonstrate them consistently and authentically become trusted entities who others will follow. By embedding the values into every conversation, interaction, and communication, organizations create a culture that will not tolerate disingenuous behaviors. Leaders who listen to understand in two-way feedback loops are respected.

The trap of micromessaging and microinequities can be avoided through willingness to anticipate our natural tendency to stereotype and categorize others. By making assumptions, we run the risk of de-activating capable people and minimizing their impact. Leaders who consciously treat employees equitably give their people the opportunity to prove their capability.

Being predisposed to asking the right questions rather than expecting to have all the answers keeps us curious and open to new possibilities. While knowledge is important for success, wisdom is far more crucial. Wise leaders ask *why* more than they ask *how*. They are willing to look for alternate solutions, and this creates a mind-set that can embrace even epic failure and learn from it.

Challenge: Be courageous in turbulent times, challenging assumptions and choosing optimism to move through change.

Leaders with tenacity garner respect. Leaders with integrity build trust. Staying true to who we are in challenging times takes courage and the ability to admit when we make mistakes. Leaders who are willing to be vulnerable, admit they don't have the answers, and ask for help empower their teams to step into a role of personal accountability. These leaders know that to succeed, they have to trust their people to do the right thing. They are allies working with their employees, not heroes taking all the glory.

Being a vulnerable leader does not mean being weak. Kind leadership shows strength by holding others accountable for results and by helping them learn and grow along the way. Change is constant, and our ability to move through fear and adapt and embrace new beginnings will determine whether we succeed or fail. Leaders who trust their teams to step into the unknown empower them to find the creativity and innovation needed to start again.

While we tend to stay at a set-point of happiness regardless of events, we have the power to build optimism through an attitude of gratitude. Optimism is not the inability to see the negative; rather it is the conscious choice to appreciate the positive and balance our perception of what happens to us. Harnessing the power of wonder can short-circuit negative emotions and reduce fear. Optimism is contagious, and leaders who demonstrate this bring others along on the journey.

Control: Move through fear and harness motivation to find the silver lining

The road to high performance is paved with choices. Leaders have the choice to be motivators or demotivators. Those who can see challenges as an opportunities to learn rather than insurmountable obstacles empower their teams to do the same.

Our world is hyperconnected, always on, and filled with distractions. But these distractions also present us with a choice. Focusing our energy on the tasks that are most important to us, and being mindful about when to tolerate distractions, enables effective prioritization and a great deal less stress. In a world of increasing distractions, consciously choosing single-tasking gives us the opportunity to engage at a deeper level with those around us, become more effective in whatever we undertake, and enjoy the satisfaction of a job well done.

Fear stifles creativity and destroys trust. Leaders who create a safe environment for innovation and encourage their people to take risks without fear of retribution can avoid the stagnation and mediocrity that comes from a toxic culture. Being able to acknowledge fear but move forward in spite of it takes leaders who know when to ask for help, can accept it with grace, and are willing to offer help in return.

Among all the attributes of great leaders, one stands above the rest: they are highly trusted. Resilient cultures are built on trust, and trust affects a leader's impact and the company's bottom line more than anything else. Trust doesn't come with the nameplate on a leader's door. It is earned over time, through compassion, consistency, integrity, and commitment to deliver.

Commit to the journey by renewing resources to nurture recovery

Athletes know that they constantly have to challenge their bodies, pushing a little farther each day as they get stronger and fitter. Building resilience is no different than building a muscle; it takes practice, persistence, and grit, despite inevitable setbacks. Resilience is not something that happens overnight. The key is to practice self-compassion when we hit an obstacle, taking the time to pick ourselves up and continue the journey.

Nurturing our physical recovery is crucial to renewing our resources and buffering against stress. Being aware of our breathing enables us to generate energy and focus our minds, resulting not only in increased productivity but also the beneficial activation of the parasympathetic nervous system.

Spending focused time with no agenda helps open up channels of creativity and innovation. And optimizing sleep patterns, moving often, and eating mindfully all serve to boost our immune system and improve our quality of life.

A LAST GLANCE AT FIVE TRUTHS

1. Change is the new constant

We live in a world of constant change. Digital transformation is changing organizations faster than any other industrial revolution before it. As we stand on the brink of the technological revolution, it is fundamentally altering the way we work, live, and relate to each other. An unprecedented convergence of people, of information, of markets coming together is disrupting not only business models in every industry, but also the way in which we engage with each other and with any kind of product or service.

It's more than just a technological revolution; every part of life, work and business is being transformed. Knowing that we're evolving at an exponential rather than at a linear pace helps us to understand that everybody is dealing with the same rate of change. The velocity and scope of that change is creating a new opportunity to deliver value to our customers at an unprecedented scale. It is also demanding that we engage with our friends, family, colleagues, and fellow human beings in an entirely different way. As our world gets smaller, we have an opportunity to create more personal connections, building relationships based on trust. This is how we navigate the human side of change—looking at it as an opportunity rather than a threat and moving through it to emerge on the other side both wiser and kinder.

2. Stress is a necessary part of our lives

Although stress and anxiety are increasingly becoming issues at work and at home, stress is actually necessary in order to function. Stress entices the brain into growing new memory cells as it releases activation hormones that allow us to perform at our peak.

The paradox of stress is that if it continues for prolonged periods (chronic stress), the opposite effect occurs, suppressing our ability to perform and shutting down the growth of memory cells. Finding the sweet spot for high performance means using the activation that comes from stress to our advantage, while short-circuiting the hard-wired fight-flight-freeze response that signals a negative response to it. This requires a shift in mind-set and a new perspective on the challenges that life throws at us.

3. Resilience takes reinforcement

Dr. Martin Luther King, Jr. said, "The ultimate measure of a man is not where he stands in moments of comfort and convenience, but where he stands in times of challenge and controversy."

It's easy to be optimistic, upbeat, and positive when things are going well. When we're having a tough day, however, resilience can be more challenging. Consciously shifting our perspective to create optimistic neural pathways takes repetition, practice, and persistence. By shifting our focus to the positive, we can change our perspective to take a longer view of any situation.

In spite of communication challenges, issues with co-workers, increased competition in the marketplace, and the myriad demands of work and life, building resilience over time helps us to pick ourselves up and carry on in the face of adversity. Neurons that fire together wire together—the more we practice resilience and nurture our recovery from stress, the more natural it becomes to have an optimistic, forward-thinking outlook, and the more capable we are of overcoming fear and moving forward in spite of it.

4. Take care of yourself first

The reality is that unless we take care of ourselves, we cannot take care of others. When we are busy we often forget to nurture our own recovery from stress through intentional focus on both mind and body. Leaders dealing with challenging transformation in every aspect of business increasingly fall prey to stress as a result, rendering them less capable of leading effectively as their health suffers.

Paying attention to our emotional and physical response to stressors enables us to proactively nurture recovery. Stress is not going anywhere. The key is to pay attention to our response to it, shift our perspective to be able to deal constructively with it, and then help others to do the same.

5. The sabertooth is a kitten

Building resilience is not an isolated activity, and for each of us, the journey will look different. But we all have the capability to use the approaches and ideas we've talked about in this book to face our own sabertooth, whatever form it takes.

In his book *Healing the Masculine Soul*, Gordon Dalby, author and graduate of Duke, Stanford, and Harvard universities, tells the story of a man who had a terrifying recurrent dream. In the man's nightmare, a ferocious male lion chased him until he dropped from exhaustion, and then he awoke screaming.

The man told his counselor about his dreams, assuming that they represented something fearful in his life. The counselor gave the man some advice: the next time he had the dream, he should confront the lion and ask what it was doing in his dream.

Before long, the man had the dream again. He wanted badly to run, but despite his fear, he stood firm. He watched in terror as the lion approached him, shaking its massive head and baring enormous white fangs. Trembling, the man asked, "Who are you? Why are you chasing me?"

The lion replied, "I am your courage. Why are you running from me?"

Finding the courage to take back control and become more confident in stressful situations takes a shift in perspective. It means stepping over the line and facing the sabertooth. If we can face it, we can tame it—and by taming it, we may find that, in reality, our sabertooth is a just a kitten.

A NOTE FROM THE AUTHOR

Life shrinks or expands in proportion
to one's courage.
—Anais Nin

I hope that you have found the stories, ideas, and suggestions in this book helpful. Thank you for walking with me through this experience, and for being open to a new way of looking at the world. Facing our sabertooth takes courage, and courage takes vulnerability. Some days will be more difficult than others. But always remember: it is in the persevering that we grow. If we have the courage to stand firm when we can't control or predict the outcome, we can face our fear and overcome it.

Above all, stepping over the line and into battle takes an ability to overcome our inner critic and to be forgiving of ourselves when we inevitably stumble. Theodore Roosevelt put it well:

> *It is not the critic who counts; not the man who points out*
> *how the strong man stumbles, or where the doer of deeds*
> *could have done them better. The credit belongs to the man*
> *who is actually in the arena, whose face is marred by dust and*
> *sweat and blood; who strives valiantly; who errs, who comes*

short again and again … who at the best knows in the end
the triumph of high achievement, and who at the worst, if he
fails, at least fails while daring greatly.

I believe that if we can embrace the messy imperfection that makes us human and be open to exploring a new approach to the way we engage with the world and connect with each other; we can discover an entirely new perspective and learn to thrive. And if we can change ourselves, each of us has the power to make a difference for those around us. As Mother Teresa said; "I alone cannot change the world, but I can cast a stone across the waters to create many ripples." I wish you all the best on your journey as you cast your stone across the water, and, finally, I hope that the words of Bob Seger will inspire you to weather any storm.

Like a Rock – Bob Seger and the Silver Bullet Band
Stood there boldly
Sweatin' in the sun
Felt like a million
Felt like number one
The height of summer
I'd never felt that strong
Like a rock …

… My hands were steady
My eyes were clear and bright
My walk had purpose
My steps were quick and light
And I held firmly
To what I felt was right
Like a rock

Like a rock, I was strong as I could be
Like a rock, nothin' ever got to me
Like a rock, I was something to see
Like a rock

And I stood arrow straight
Unencumbered by the weight
Of all these hustlers and their schemes
I stood proud, I stood tall
High above it all
I still believed in my dreams …

… And sometimes late at night
When I'm bathed in the firelight
The moon comes callin' a ghostly white
And I recall
I recall

Like a rock, standin' arrow straight
Like a rock, chargin' from the gate
Like a rock, carryin' the weight
Like a rock

Like a rock, the sun upon my skin
Like a rock, hard against the wind
Like a rock, I see myself again
Like a rock

ACKNOWLEDGEMENTS

I always knew I would write this book, even though it has taken about a decade of false starts and scribbles on sticky notes as I pieced it all together. There have been many friends and colleagues along the way who offered the thoughts and stories that have found their way into this book. I have to thank so many of you whom I have worked with over the years on three continents. We've gone out to battle side by side, weathering the storm of business changes, setbacks, and successes, and shared invaluable lessons along the way.

I am grateful to the multitude of authors, academics, and practitioners whose work has directly inspired my own. In particular, the psychology department at Eastern Washington University and the incredible group of colleagues and coaches at Fielding Graduate University. The lessons I learned all those years ago served as the foundation on which this book is built and I owe you a debt of gratitude.

To my circle of friends, my life is so much richer because of each of you. Your openness to delving into your own experience and offering perceptions of your workplace gave substance and meaning to the ideas I was cultivating. Your encouragement to finish what I started helped me to keep going when I doubted that I could stay the course.

Kelly Smith and Eland Mann, my editorial collaborators at Advantage, thank you for coaching, advising, and, when necessary, prodding me with your perspective and wisdom throughout all the stages of the manuscript. Thank you also for sharing your own inspirational stories. Your enthusiasm for the ideas in the book continually stirred my thinking and reminded me of the reasons I started in the first place. To Carly Blake, for making the book look beautiful, thank you. To the entire team at Advantage who held my hand throughout the publishing process (and patiently answered my endless questions), thank you for keeping me motivated and giving me the final push over the finish line.

I especially want to thank my clients, past and present—you have provided me daily opportunities to learn, grow, and be a better collaborator and coach. My experiences with you gave me the ingredients to pull together what I believe is a story worth telling. I have told it as best I can.

Most of all, thank you to my husband, Peter. I finally got it done, can you believe it? Thank you for walking beside me through the demands of writing, and for offering both wise insights and helpful edits. You inspire me to be better every day. Without you cheering me on, this book would not have happened.

ABOUT THE AUTHOR

Tracey Grove is a high-performance coach specializing in leadership effectiveness and executive coaching. She founded Pure Symmetry in 2008 with the intention of helping people and organizations thrive. With over two decades of experience across both public and private sectors working on three continents, Tracey has benefited deeply from dealing with individual and interpersonal issues, communication challenges, and organizational shifts. She has taught the skill of resilience to thousands in over twenty countries around the world.

She leverages organizational psychology, neuroscience, cognitive behavioral and positive psychology approaches to help clients break down patterns of behavior that do not serve them well. She applies communication and organizational relationship theories to help both individuals and leaders to have authentic conversations, empowering them and others to succeed.

Tracey has dedicated the past two decades of her life to developing resilient leaders and organizations that are adaptable to a rapidly changing environment. She holds a master's in organizational development and leadership from Fielding Graduate University and is accredited by the International Coach Federation as a professional certified coach.

Tracey lives in Washington State in the United States with her husband. Outside of work, she can be found curled up on the sofa indulging her love of a good book on a rainy day or whipping up something delicious in the kitchen over a glass of fine wine, in good company.

OUR SERVICES

If you enjoyed *Taming the Sabertooth*, download the Pure Symmetry app for inspiration, tips, and reminders for building resilience and leading with courage. Visit puresymmetry.com/app.html.

For speaker inquiries, email info@puresymmetry.com.

Visit puresymmetry.com to learn more about individual and group executive coaching. Executive coaching benefits individuals and organizations in five key areas:

- Improved collaboration and conflict management.

- Clarity in communication and personal presence.

- Increased productivity and ability to overcome obstacles.

- Increased engagement and reduced attrition.

- Enhanced adaptability, resilience, and performance.

Connect with Tracey on LinkedIn at linkedin.com/in/traceygrove. Follow her on Twitter at twitter.com/traceygrove.

CPSIA information can be obtained
at www.ICGtesting.com
Printed in the USA
JSHW041713120521
14656JS00001B/54